Prayerful: How the Scriptures, History, and Experience Can Shape Our Prayers

Copyright © 2024 by Todd von Helms. All rights reserved.
Published by Truth Matters Press.

Cover and interior design by Useful Group

Scripture quotations taken from The Holy Bible, New International Version® NIV®
Copyright © 1973 1978 1984 2011 by Biblica, Inc.TM
Used by permission. All rights reserved worldwide.

Cover photo: Jordan Steranka

ISBN: 979-8-218-36499-1 (paperback)

PRAYERFUL

How *the* Scriptures, History, *and* Experience
Can Shape Our Prayers

to Raymond,
Grace + peace to you!
Todd von Helms

TODD VON HELMS

Contents

Foreword	1
Chapter 1: Introduction	3
Chapter 2: To Whom Do We Pray?	9
Chapter 3: The Triune God Helps Us Pray	15
Chapter 4: Honest Prayer	21
Chapter 5: Prayer is Our Holy Occupation	25
Chapter 6: God Always Hears Our Prayers	29
Chapter 7: God's Timing and Responses to Our Prayers (Yes, No, Wait)	33
Chapter 8: The Problem of Sin	37
Chapter 9: Prayer and the Seven Deadly Sins	41
Chapter 10: Confession and Prayer	47
Chapter 11: Praying for Wisdom and Discernment	53
Chapter 12: Praying with Right Motives	59
Chapter 13: Humility and Prayer	65
Chapter 14: Praying with Thanksgiving	69
Chapter 15: Praying Through Trials	73

Chapter 16: Turning Worry into Prayer	79
Chapter 17: Meditating on and Praying Scripture (Lectio Divina)	85
Chapter 18: The Lord's Prayer	91
Chapter 19: Praying the Psalms	95
Chapter 20: Prayers of Lament	99
Chapter 21: Free and Formed Prayers	105
Chapter 22: Praying for Others	111
Chapter 23: Praying for Enemies	115
Chapter 24: Keeping a Prayer Journal	119
Chapter 25: The Importance of Silence, Solitude, and a Place to Pray	123
Chapter 26: Time to Pray	129
Chapter 27: Fasting and Other Aids to Prayer	133
Chapter 28: Praying for Healing	139
Chapter 29: Praying for Revival	145
Chapter 30: Praying with Eternity in Mind	149

Foreword

Blake Holmes, Lead Pastor
Watermark Community Church, Dallas, TX

Prayer is a gift from God. So, why is it when the subject of prayer comes up, many people feel confused, guilty, embarrassed, or even ashamed? Perhaps you want to pray but simply don't know how. If that is you, then this book is for you! Let my friend, Todd von Helms, thoughtfully and respectfully walk you through some of the commonly asked questions about prayer. To whom do we pray? How do we know God really hears our prayers? How can we pray through worry, fear, stress, sin, and doubt? How should we pray about decisions? What is the value of keeping a prayer journal? How can prayer become a consistent, powerful way of life, especially when busy, distracted, and at times just trying to survive? This book addresses each of these questions and so much more!

While avoiding formulaic answers and cliches, this guide will expand your understanding of prayer and possibly challenge your preconceptions as well. Wherever you are on your spiritual journey, I'm confident you will be encouraged as you read numerous examples from the scriptures and history about how you can strengthen your relationship with God and others through prayer.

My word of encouragement to you is to not race through this short book, but read it slowly and carefully consider the insights offered. Or, even better, grab a small group of friends and discuss what the Lord reveals to you.

CHAPTER 1
Introduction

A simple investigation of prayer reveals that there are many different ways to pray. Some pray aloud, while others pray silently. Most pray only with heads bowed and eyes closed, while some pray with their eyes open (even if that seems weird). Some pray while walking or running, while others pray on their knees. Some pray only scripture or prescribed prayers, whereas others insist on praying spontaneously. Many pray in the morning or only before meals, while others prefer praying before bedtime. Some pray multiple times every day, while others struggle to pray at all.

How can something as seemingly simple as prayer produce such a diversity of opinions? I've heard it said that there is no wrong way to pray, as long as one is sincere. During college, a lady in front of me at a convenience store purchased a lottery ticket and said to the cashier, "You can't be blessed if you don't play, and you better be sure to pray about getting the winning numbers!" She was serious, and I left wondering if the odds of winning might increase for people praying to win the jackpot.

Over the years I've watched television preachers promise viewers who pray and send enough money to the address on the screen that God will multiply their donations and send them blessings in return. Based on the millions of dollars that pour into television preachers each year, thousands of people must believe in the sincerity of their messages and theology.

Prayerful

Growing up, I remember how my coaches and teams prayed together before every public high school basketball game. For that matter, prayers were sometimes offered on the PA system before games. Unbeknownst to me, at the time prayer was simply part of the culture. Following the games that our team lost, I wondered if the other side had more people praying for them, or if they were just the better team that night. The same questions cross my mind when I hear coaches and athletes during postgame interviews thanking God for allowing their team to win the game.

I also recall the theme of prayer showing up in many movies along the way, from the heights of *Forrest Gump* and the epic *Star Wars* series to the depths of Ricky Bobby offering a jumbled prayer with his family before a meal in *Talladega Nights*. Perhaps the strangest movie scene I remember took place in Oliver Stone's biographical film about the rock-n-roll band, The Doors. During a particular scene at a party, eccentric pop artist Andy Warhol hands Jim Morrison, the band's iconic lead singer, a golden telephone. As he hands the phone to Morrison, Warhol says, "Someone gave me this telephone... She said I could talk to God with it, but I don't have anything to say. Here, this is for you. Now you can talk to God." Warhol seemed to believe one could actually talk to God using a telephone, thus adding to the list of different beliefs about prayer.

Though ideas about prayer can vary drastically, there has always been a universal longing for humans to communicate with some type of god or "Higher Power." On one hand, it seems both incredible and audacious to think that a mighty Creator of the entire universe would care to communicate with lowly creatures. But on the other hand, if God created and sustains everything, then the concept of prayer makes perfect sense. For after all, why wouldn't a Creator want to communicate with creatures? If not, then why bother creating humans in the first place? The fact that we exist at all is quite miraculous.

Introduction

I know few people who would not admit to believing in a spiritual realm or some type of god. Mankind has always been religious, and prayer is part of every religion. Prayer is the chief means by which billions of religious people attempt to connect to their respective god. Cultural background often shapes our prayers, and it is common to hear adults reciting prayers learned during childhood. Jews are required to recite the *Shema* twice per day: "Hear O Israel: The Lord our God, the Lord is one" (Deuteronomy 6:4). They're also instructed to pray facing Jerusalem, which was modeled by the prophet Daniel who opened windows facing the Holy City as he prayed several times each day (Daniel 6:10-28). Muslims are commanded to pray five times per day facing Mecca. Many Native Americans pray facing the four cardinal directions of the earth in order to connect with nature and the Creator. Perhaps particular childhood or cultural influences have shaped your prayers?

Both statistics and observation demonstrate that most people pray. A recent national survey showed this to be true. In fact, 55% of adults pray every day, with 20% of that group claiming no formal religious affiliation.[1] At some point in life, everyone prays, even if only when facing a crisis. I was reminded of this not long ago while watching a professional American football game.

During a nationally televised NFL game between the Buffalo Bills and Cincinnati Bengals, players and fans in attendance, as well as millions of online viewers, witnessed a never-seen-before tragedy unfold in real time. During the second half of the game, defensive player Damar Hamlin of the Buffalo Bills collided with another player, suffered cardiac arrest and collapsed on the field. His heart had stopped, and every second mattered as paramedics performed CPR in an attempt to save Damar's life. The facial expressions and

---

[1] "Frequency of Prayer." *Pew Research Center*, https://www.pewforum.org/religious-landscape-study/frequency-of-prayer. Accessed December 23, 2023.

body language of teammates and opponents alike demonstrated the severity of the situation. Religious differences and political correctness didn't matter, nor did broadcasting protocols or agendas. People from all walks of life came together to pray for Damar's survival, including commentators, coaches, cheerleaders, and even the fans rooting against Damar's team. The football game with playoff implications no longer mattered and the game was rightly canceled.

In the ensuing days, people around the world prayed for Damar Hamlin. Thankfully, in what many have labeled miraculous, Damar recovered. He is grateful to be alive and happy to be playing football again. Though it is impossible to know the religious belief or conception of God held in the mind of each person who prayed for Damar, it is obvious that extraordinary situations cause everyone to realize the need for prayer.

According to the Hebrew scriptures, the longing to connect with someone or something beyond our tangible world results from humans being made in the image of God (Genesis 1:26). According to Thomas Aquinas, the greatest theologian of the Middle Ages, prayer is "an expression of man's desire for God." Nineteenth century British minister Charles Spurgeon described prayer as "the soul talking to God."[2] Influential theologian Robert Barron explained prayer as "the coming together of our longing for God and God's longing for us."[3] Regardless of how it's defined, people connect to God through prayer. It is simple enough for a child, yet sometimes difficult for the most mature believers.

Teaching someone to pray is similar to teaching someone how to fall in love. Success is not guaranteed, and no one can learn to pray or fall in love without trying. There is not a magic formula or one

---

[2] Charles Spurgeon. *The Power in Prayer*. (New Kensington, PA: Whitaker House, 1996), 170.

[3] Robert Barron. *Catholicism: A Journey to the Heart of Faith*. (New York: Image, 2011), 225.

size fits all approach to prayer, but without considering time-proven methods that have enabled generations of believers to connect with God, most people simply do not know how to start or continue praying. We do not first learn how to pray and then proceed to pray. Rather, through praying we find out what we are doing, and then deepen and mature in our praying.[4]

Talking about God and prayer are not the same as talking to God through prayer. I've been to "prayer meetings" that involved more talking to others about God than talking to God about others. Prayer is something we do. It is not about religiosity, but a relationship between lowly creatures and the Almighty Creator who knows us best and loves us most. Like all healthy relationships, having one with God requires time, commitment, effort, persistence, patience, and a lot of grace. The communication must be sincere and include both talking and listening. In addition to the Bible, prayer is the chief means by which we can know and communicate with God and receive the wisdom and strength needed to fulfill his purposes in and through our lives. The two go hand in hand, and that's why much of this book uses the scriptures as the authoritative guide regarding prayer.

Because each person is different, a variety of approaches to prayer should be considered. Scripture and history provide many great examples to emulate; hence the subtitle of this book, "How the Scriptures, History, and Experience Can Shape Our Prayers." Many suggestions are provided throughout, and it will be up to each reader to decide which ones to disregard or adopt over the course of the next 30 days (for those wanting to use the book as a daily devotional for a month) or during the course of 5-6 weeks if an individual or group desires to read a chapter per day for five or six days per week. Some may want to walk through the book during the Advent or Lent season.

---

[4] Eugene H. Peterson. *Answering God: The Psalms as Tools for Prayer*. (New York: HarperCollins, 1989), 35.

Prayerful

The key to becoming a more prayerful person is to get started and not give up. Praying may not always change our circumstances, but we will always be changed for the better when we encounter God through prayer. Becoming a prayerful person will not happen overnight. In fact, it is a lifetime endeavor. My hope is that you will learn to embrace prayer, not as a method, but as a way of life. My prayer is that this book will draw you closer to God, enrich your prayer life, and increase your love for God and others.

CHAPTER 2
To Whom Do We Pray?

How one thinks about God will determine the way in which he or she prays, or if the person prays at all. A small perception of God will result in a weak or non-existent prayer life, whereas a proper view of God's character and nature will result in a healthy approach to prayer. Those who do not believe in God seldom sense a desire or reason to pray, for if God does not exist, why bother praying? Those who have encountered God usually respond with prayer. Those who realize their need for grace and forgiveness cannot help but pray.

Though God is mysterious, the scriptures provide us what we need to know about his nature and attributes. God is all-knowing (omniscient), all-powerful (omnipotent), present everywhere (omnipresent), always just, and always doing what is best for his glory and children. He is unchanging, always faithful, and full of love, mercy, and grace. Every good and perfect thing comes from the Lord. He is the holy Creator and Sustainer of all things, including our prayers.

Though we attempt to describe that which our finite human words ultimately cannot, we can be confident in the fact that God has revealed to us through nature in general, and through the inspired words of the scriptures in particular, everything we need to know. The Bible says, "Since the creation of the world God's invisible qualities—his eternal power and divine nature—have been clearly seen, being understood from what has been made" (Romans 1:20).

I truly grasped the meaning of this passage through encountering God in nature on two separate occasions.

I had heard about the Grand Canyon since childhood. It seemed impressive based on the pictures I had seen, but eyewitnesses assured me that my second-hand knowledge was nothing like experiencing it personally. Last summer, I was given the opportunity to see what was so great about the Grand Canyon. Once inside the park, signs led me down a pathway to see what I had been anticipating for many years. As the vast canyon initially came into view, I noticed my youngest son, who had run ahead of me, standing along the edge with his arms raised in victory as if he had hit his first home run. When my eyes finally beheld the majestic, almost indescribable beauty of the Grand Canyon, all I could say was, "Wow!" It was breathtaking to say the least.

Another experience in nature that left me awestruck happened late one night while sitting on the deck of a boat in the middle of the ocean near the Galapagos Islands. These remote islands are located about two hours west of Ecuador and are some of the most beautiful and uninhabited parts of the world. It was so dark on the deck of the boat that I couldn't see my hand placed a few inches from my face. When I looked up at the night sky, however, millions of stars could be seen. Not only could I pick out every famous constellation, but the rare opportunity to see the North Star and Southern Cross at the same time was also possible given our close proximity to the Equator.

For hours I marveled at the beauty of nature on full display, just as I had done while observing the Grand Canyon. In both places, I remember thinking, *"How can anyone who sees this doubt the existence of a Creator?"* I also thought about how some might say, "We cannot see God." Well, visit the Grand Canyon or Galapagos Islands and your opinion will likely change. We cannot see the wind, but we can feel it. I could see and feel God's presence as I stood and walked along on the edge of the Grand Canyon. Likewise, countless stars reside in the heavens every night, but it took being on the deck of a boat in the middle of the ocean to see them for the first time. They were there all along, just as God is.

In both places, my view and understanding of God were clearer, and it had everything to do with being in a context conducive to experiencing God. Several passages of scripture also came to mind that night:

> The heavens declare the glory of God. The skies display his marvelous craftmanship. Day after day they continue to speak, night after night they make him known (Psalm 19:1-2).

> God determines the number of stars and calls them each by name (Psalm 147:4).

Nature truly points us to a Creator! Imagine how much greater is the One who created it all! God's handiwork is on full display in places like the Grand Canyon and Galapagos Islands. You can see pictures, and hear stories like mine, but you need to experience them personally to really understand and appreciate the beauty and greatness of these magnificent places. The same applies to God. You must encounter God personally. Though God has clearly revealed himself in nature, the holy scriptures and prayer enable people to know and commune with God on an intimate level.

Understanding to whom we pray is as important as praying itself, for we cannot worship God properly if we do not understand who God is. Christianity is about the triune God (God the Father, God the Son, God the Holy Spirit). Not three gods, for that is polytheism, but three persons in one essence. It's been said to think of the triune God as $1 \times 1 \times 1 = 1$. The word "Trinity" was allegedly coined by an early church leader named Tertullian in the second century, and it has been the common term used to describe the triune God ever since.

The Father, Son, and Holy Spirit have always existed as the Trinity. The Bible reveals that the triune God created everything, including the heavens, Earth, humans, and all other creatures. This means that

Prayerful

Jesus did not just show up 2,000 years ago but has always existed. The first verses of John's Gospel explain it this way: "In the beginning was the Word, and the Word was with God, and the Word was God. Through him [Christ] all things were made" (John 1:1-3). The apostle Paul declared, "Christ is the image of the invisible God, the firstborn over all creation. For by him all things were created: things in heaven and on earth, visible and invisible, whether thrones or powers or rulers or authorities; all things were created by him and for him. He is before all things, and in him all things hold together" (Colossians 1:15-17). Christ was and is the Word of God (the Logos) who created and sustains all things.

Though the triune God is the transcendent Creator of all things, he is also personal because Jesus is a person (God in the flesh). God the Father and God the Holy Spirit are personal as well. Following centuries of mankind trying to reach for, understand, and even appease God for the guilt of sins, at just the right time, the Word (Jesus) became flesh to rescue humanity from their sins (Galatians 4:4). Jesus, who created us out of love, decided to enter his creation as a creature (being fully God and fully human). It is the reason why Christians celebrate the birth of Christ at Christmas every year. The angels announced that Emmanuel, which means "God with us," had come. In perhaps the most well-known verse in the Bible, the apostle John explains: "For God so loved the world that he gave his one and only Son, that whoever believes in him shall not perish but have eternal life" (John 3:16).

Jesus, the Messiah, had arrived in the form of a humble servant, being born in the likeness of men. One title used for Jesus is "Son of God," which means He is God (John 5:18). Jesus, the "Christ," is the essence of Christianity because he made the invisible visible, thus enabling us to have the best view of the triune God. This is why Jesus said, "Anyone who has seen me has seen the Father" (John 14:9). In another place, Jesus declared, "I and the Father are one" (John 10:30).

The Bible also says, "The Father loves the Son and has placed everything in his hands" (John 3:35). Jesus did things only God the Father could do, like judge and forgive sins and raise people from the dead (John 1:3; 5:21-22). This is also why Jesus said, "No one knows the Father except the Son and those to whom the Son enables to understand" (Matthew 11:27). As a final exclamation point about being God incarnate, Jesus said, "I am the way, the truth, and the life. No one comes to the Father except through me" (John 14:6). Christ enables every believer to experience the mysterious, unfathomable love of the Trinity.

Not only did Jesus, the only begotten Son of God, provide clear instructions about how one can know God personally, he also promised to send the Holy Spirit to empower and guide his followers to pray and live as they should. Notice the promise made by Jesus to his earliest followers:

> If you love me, keep my commands. And I will ask the Father, and he will give you another advocate to help you and be with you forever— the Spirit of truth. The world cannot accept him, because it neither sees him nor knows him. But you know him, for he lives with you and will be in you (John 14:15-17).

The promised Holy Spirit arrived after the resurrection and ascension of Jesus to empower his followers in a mighty way (Acts 2). What's even more remarkable is that we can experience the same power of the Holy Spirit today as he continues working in the lives of believers right now. Jesus said, "the heavenly Father will give the Holy Spirit to those who ask him" (Luke 11:13). The Bible proclaims that God's Spirit dwells in everyone who places his or her complete trust in God (1 Cor 3:16). Though Christ is seated at the right hand of God, the Holy Spirit is present with us at every moment. How comforting to know that the same power, grace, and love of the Holy Spirit that indwelled the early Church also works in and through Christ's Church today![5] The apostle Paul wrote a beautiful reminder of this reality:

> In all these things we are more than conquerors through him who loved us. For I am convinced that neither death nor life, neither angels nor demons, neither the present nor the future, nor any powers, neither height nor depth, nor anything else in all creation, will be able to separate us from the love of God that is in Christ Jesus our Lord (Romans 8:37-39).

Prayer and Bible reading are like windows or doors that invite the wisdom and power of the Holy Spirit into our daily lives. Our formal relationship with the triune God starts with a prayer, and our daily commitment to reading the Bible and praying enables us to fulfill God's purposes in and through our lives.

Questions for Reflection

What are some of the adjectives that come to mind when you think of God?

Do you believe that your view of God affects your ability and desire to pray?

---

[5] For a concise overview, see R.C. Sproul's book, *The Mystery of the Holy Spirit*.

CHAPTER 3
The Triune God Helps Us Pray

We may know very little about God, but he knows everything about us. Despite our limited understanding of God or feeble efforts to pray, God delights in watching us mature in faith and learning how to communicate through prayer.

Our spiritual development can be similar to that of our physical development, which includes learning how to talk. There are few things more enjoyable than witnessing a baby speak words for the first time. The words ball, momma, or dada become music to a parent's ears. There are hundreds of variants of grandpa and grandma out there thanks to a baby's initial failed attempts to say those names correctly. The mispronounced words stick because we cherish the baby's first attempts to communicate. No one is disappointed with a baby's effort.

I can imagine that the heavenly Father is just as pleased with those in the infant stages of faith simply trying to communicate through prayer. God desires to hear from us because he created us and loves us. With experience, we can learn to communicate with God more effectively.

Even during the best of times, life can present various challenges. As we are learning how to make prayer a consistent part of life, obstacles can prevent us from praying as we should. This has always been the case, even for those living when Jesus walked the Earth during the first century. In his letter to the church in Rome, the apostle Paul wrote, "We do not know what we ought to pray for" (Romans 8:26). Likewise, one of Christ's closest followers once said, "Lord, teach us to pray" (Luke 11:1).

No matter how overwhelming life can become, God is always available to help us through prayer. The Bible mentions the story of a desperate father who brought his son to Jesus for healing. When Jesus asked the father if he believed his son could be healed, the father said, "I do believe; help me overcome my unbelief" (Mark 9:23-25). Perhaps you've asked God to help you overcome a stressful situation. Perhaps you wanted to ask God for help, but simply felt too overwhelmed with fear, doubt, or guilt to pray. Rather than turning to God, it seemed easier to rely on someone or something else to fix the problem or numb the pain.

I've known people who spent many years trying to find purpose and meaning in life apart from God. Within each of us is a longing to feel accepted and loved. You've probably heard the expression, "We should love others as we love ourselves." Unfortunately, if we don't love ourselves, we will have a hard time loving other people as we should. We cannot love ourselves or others until we realize how much God loves us. Prayer enables us to bask in the rays of God's perfect, unending love.

Many people want to pray but simply don't know how. Some refuse to pray because they do not believe God exists. Others refrain from praying because they do not think God really cares about their lives. I've met some people who didn't pray because they believed God was too angry and disappointed to listen to their prayers. The guilt and shame that accompanied their bad choices made prayer seem impossible. I was reminded of this during an unexpected encounter a couple years ago. It was my second time to speak to a group of mostly retired Christians at a country club located on a beach in North Carolina. On this occasion, a group of twelve women, mostly in their late teens and early twenties, walked in and sat down just before I started speaking. Many in the group sported tattoos and piercings and didn't seem to fit in with the crowd. Though some of the mainstays seemed a little perplexed by the younger visitors, I was thrilled to see them there.

As I talked about God's unconditional love and amazing grace, I noticed a few of these young ladies starting to cry, especially as I shared about God loving us despite our failures. The reality is that no matter how good or bad we may view ourselves to be, we are likely far worse. That's the bad news. The good news is that God's love and grace are much more powerful than anyone's sin. There is nothing we can ever do to make God love us more or less than he always has; even more than that, his free gift of grace is always available. Grace is unmerited favor, which means it doesn't matter what you've accomplished, how much money you have, who your parents are, how badly you've messed up, or if you are a member of a country club. Anyone can receive God's unconditional love and free gift of grace at any time. As I finished my message, two of the girls came up to speak with me.

> I said, "I'm so glad you are here. Are you members of this country club?"

> They said, "No, we've never been to a country club."
> I then asked if they were part of a church group, to which they replied, "No, we don't go to church either." Knowing they came in together, I asked, "I saw you come in as a group. Are you part of an organization?"

> One girl said, "We are drug addicts living in a halfway house nearby. We are here today because an older lady visited the rehab house and invited us this morning. She said we could get away and enjoy a free lunch at this country club, so here we are."

Incredulous, I said, "Wow, that's amazing! It's so cool that you're here today! I noticed during my sermon that you both seemed to be a little emotional. Was it something I said?"

One girl started crying and said, "I just can't believe God really loves me despite all I've done. I've messed up so badly."

I said, "God not only loves you, but he cherishes you and has a plan for your life. He loves you the way you are, not as you should be, because no one is as they should be. If you confess your sins, God will forgive you. Can I pray for you?"

"Yes! I'd like that," she said. When we finished praying, the young woman said, "That's the first time I've prayed in years." When I asked why, she said, "I've felt too guilty to pray." I then said to her, "God will always forgive you when you sincerely ask for forgiveness and help. He will also help you to pray, even when you feel as though you cannot."

It is hard to explain how much that conversation blessed me. I provided my contact information hoping I'd hear from someone.

A year later, I attended a wedding that took place in that same beach town. On the way home, my wife and I stopped at a restaurant for dinner. As we were paying the bill, a waitress stopped at our table and said to me, "I think I know you. Are you a minister?" I chuckled and said, "Sometimes." She then said, "I knew it was you. I heard you speak at a country club with some of my friends last summer. We were living in a rehab house. Thank you for telling us about God's amazing love and grace. And thank you for praying with us. I've been sober, working, going to school, and praying every day. You were right, God helped me when I turned to him."

I was so taken aback by this news that I had trouble speaking. Through tears of joy, I said, "I can't tell you how much this means to me. Thank you for sharing. I'm so proud of you. God is good, and you are living proof of his goodness."

It is amazing to know that the One who created and knows the billions of stars by name, knew and loved us even before we were born. It's not coincidental that a group of drug addicts showed up at a country club to hear me speak a couple years ago. God also knew that I would just so happen to run into one of the girls at a restaurant a year later. I am often reminded of God's sovereignty. He truly knows every detail of our lives, including the number of days in which each of us will live. There is never a moment when we are not in the presence of God! No matter how alone we might feel, we are never alone. Take a moment to reflect on this comforting reality described in Psalm 139:

> O Lord, you have searched me and you know me. You know when I sit and when I rise; you perceive my thoughts from afar. You discern my going out and my lying down; you are familiar with all my ways. Before a word is on my tongue you know it completely, O Lord (verses 1-4).

> For You created my inmost being; you knit me together in my mother's womb. I praise you because I am fearfully and wonderfully made (verses 13-14).

> All the days ordained for me were written in your book before one of them came to be (verse 16).

Isn't it comforting to know that the sovereign God of all creation has been with you at every moment of your life? He knew you before you were born, while you were in your mother's womb, and when you entered this noisy world. He was with you yesterday, and he is with you now, even while you read this book. God knows everything you've ever said and done, and he loves you more than you can imagine.

Prayerful

Just like the young lady in the story I described earlier, there will be times in life when you may not have the faith or energy needed to pray. God knew this would be the case, and that is why we can be assured that Christ and the Holy Spirit will help us in our weakness and greatest times of need (John 16:4-15; Romans 8:26-34).

The Bible declares that Christ is our representative before God (Acts 7:55-56; Romans 8:34; Ephesians 1:20; Colossians 3:1). The apostle Paul reminds us that, "Christ Jesus, who was raised to life is at the right hand of God interceding for us." At the same time, the Spirit also helps us to pray. How awesome to know that Jesus Christ and the Holy Spirit are interceding for us! When we pray to God, through Christ, we are actually joining Christ in prayer. As Christians, we can always take comfort in the fact that the triune God is with us at every moment and wants to help us pray.

Questions for Reflection

Why does God want to hear from us?

Psalm 139 mentions that God knew us before we were born and knows every detail of our lives. It also mentions that God is in complete control. How should these truths inform and shape our prayers?

CHAPTER 4
Honest Prayer

My friend Robert, who is a little cynical about Christians, has often said, "Too many believers I've known put on a happy face, but I know their real stories. They're like parents who argue in the car on the way to church, even in the parking lot, and then step inside the building, smile, and tell everyone how greatly God has blessed their marriage. So many Christians wouldn't say the word "crap" in public even if they were standing in a pile of manure. They might fool themselves and everyone else, but God sees and hears everything. Life is too short to be around phony Christians!"

Bono, the lead singer of the famous rock band U2, himself a follower of Christ, once said, "I am suspicious of some Christians because they lack realism. What God wants is the truth." Bono is exactly right. As we pray, we must be honest with God, for he knows exactly what we've done, how we feel, and what we are thinking at all times. We cannot fool, bribe, or manipulate God with our prayers. Neither can we inform God of something he doesn't know. Being real with God helps us to be real with others too.

Life is too short to be pretenders in the Spirit. People know when we're not being honest about our lives. That's why it is so refreshing to hear people being candid about their struggles. My friend Tim wrestled with drinking for many years. Thankfully, he is now ten years sober and remains very active in Alcoholics Anonymous. He continues to meet most mornings with a group of other professionals who are also alcoholics.

According to the medical industry, an alcoholic is always an alcoholic, even if sober for many years. Thankfully, a true Christian is always a Christian, even when he or she does not act like it! One thing alcoholics and Christians have in common is the need for daily encouragement and accountability. They also need honesty and transparency in their lives.

Not a day goes by without Tim talking to God about his challenges. He also checks in with at least one of his trusted friends who prays for him daily. Every Friday morning, a group of men gather at his house. As you can imagine, I was thrilled to receive an invitation to share a devotional with the guys. I wasn't sure what to expect but am glad to report that it ended up being one of the most engaging meetings I have ever experienced, especially because of the attitude of the group.

A little before 6:00 in the morning, each of the twelve participants arrived and embraced one another with a smile, big hug, and a few derogatory nicknames. It was obvious that they were a tight-knit group that genuinely wanted to be together. Each man greeted me with warmth and a smile as well.

As our discussion unfolded, I was amazed by the transparency of the group. They knew it was okay not to be okay, and that they could be completely honest with each other. There were neither masks, nor any form of pretense of having it all together. Despite each guy being quite successful in terms of their respective jobs, no one seemed to care about titles or status. I can think of very few contexts in which people are so transparent and eager to help one another.

The meeting with the guys in AA reminded me of what the Church should be like. It also reminded me about the importance of humility and gratitude when approaching the One who knows us best and loves us most. Every person has hurts, hang ups, and wounds that have been either self-inflicted or caused by others. The guys in the recovery group that morning reminded me that God loves us despite our many flaws. Listening to their stories of brokenness and restoration was quite moving, as was our time of sharing struggles and praying together.

Two questions crossed my mind that morning that have lingered since. The first is, "Without our wounds, where would our power be?" Second, "Why do so many people struggle with pride and refuse to be part of the fellowship and accountability that is available to them?" Everyone in that group puts the interests and concerns of others before their own. These guys know the extent of their helplessness, and that simply showing up for fellowship with other sinners puts them in the best position to receive God's grace and the encouragement needed to resist their greatest temptations. I am grateful to God for allowing me to learn from a group of alcoholics what humility looks like, as well as the importance of being honest with God.

We must approach God as we actually are, not as we think we should be.[6] The guys in that AA group realize their daily need for God's grace and the support of others. Simply walking through the door to the meetings signifies as much. When we come to this realization, our communication with God and others can become more honest as well.

---

[6] Eugene H. Peterson. *Answering God: The Psalms as Tools for Prayer.* (New York: HarperCollins, 1989), 3.

Questions for Reflection

Is there someone in your life who you can be completely honest with about your temptations and struggles?

If you are not part of a group of believers, pray about and seek fellowship with people who will meet you where you are, demonstrate humility and transparency, and encourage you to live in God's grace each day.

CHAPTER 5
Prayer is Our Holy Occupation

Prayer changes things—especially the one who chooses to pray. No matter where you are in life, prayer is available at all times. It is an opportunity and privilege being able to talk to the Lord of the universe at any moment.

Prayer is also a command, given for our own good. Like a gift, it should be received, utilized and enjoyed. Like a shield, it should be used to resist the ever-present, invisible, evil forces within the cosmic realm that are often manifested in visible ways. Prayer is as essential to our spiritual life as eating is to our physical well-being. We can choose to pray or decide to be spiritually malnourished. I realize it can be easier said than done, but the benefits far outweigh the negative spiritual consequences of not praying. We will see God working through our prayers when we choose to pray.

I've heard Christians tell me that they simply do not feel like praying. I can certainly relate. No one said it would be easy. In fact, prayer is often difficult, especially at first. Pursuing anything worthwhile requires time, effort, and commitment. Prayer is no exception. Oswald Chambers, author of the best-selling devotional *My Utmost for His Highest*, defined prayer as "our holy occupation."[7] At times,

---

[7] This is the title of one of the most influential books on prayer I've ever read, also written by Chambers.

most of us feel like skipping work—even those of us who like our jobs. Perhaps you realize the importance of prayer and want it to be a significant part of your life, but feel like you're stuck in park or neutral? It can be similar to knowing the benefits of working out but refusing to go to a gym. Because it won't happen without effort, the first and most difficult step is getting started.

I remember how unnatural it was when learning how to play the guitar. My fingertips hurt when trying to hold down the strings to play, and the whole process seemed awkward at first. Yet as I kept at it, my fingers became calloused, which alleviated the pain while playing. Before long, playing the guitar seemed more natural with each passing day. In subsequent weeks I was able to strike the chords with ease and began to find much pleasure in playing. In a similar way, prayer seems very unnatural when you first get started, yet through commitment, perhaps even calloused knees, the process begins to become less like work, and more natural, spontaneous, and enjoyable.

Richard Foster, author of the classic work, *Celebration of Discipline*, explains:

> We must never wait until we feel like praying before we pray. Prayer is like any other work; we may not feel like working, but once we have been at it for a bit, we begin to feel *life* working. A pianist may not feel like playing the piano, but once he plays, he feels like doing it. In the same way, our prayer muscles need to be limbered up a bit and once the blood-flow of intercession begins, we will find that we feel like praying.[8]

I've found that anything in life worth pursuing can become challenging at times, whether it has to do with learning an instrument,

---

[8] Richard J. Foster. *Celebration of Discipline: The Path to Spiritual Growth*. (San Francisco: HarperCollins, 1998), 45.

building relationships, earning a college degree, or advancing a career. When the going gets tough, we are usually left with two options—quit or keep pressing on.

If we want to know God and his will for our lives, we must pray. If we want to become more like Christ, we must pray. If we want to love God, ourselves, and others as we should, we must pray. As John Calvin correctly pointed out, "The end of our labor in daily prayer should be to know God better. When spending time with God is the ultimate goal of prayer, choosing not to pray would be of as little profit as a man neglecting a treasure, buried and hidden in the earth, after it had been pointed out to him."[9] Keep in mind, prayer is not about asking for and receiving materialistic treasure, but realizing that every time we pray, we are conversing with the Lord of all creation. When we understand this reality, our holy occupation becomes even more valuable and enjoyable. Over time, God becomes our treasure, and we realize how much we are treasured!

God doesn't need our prayers, because he doesn't need anything. Though God doesn't need our prayers, God desires and deserves our prayers. We know God wants to hear from us because he has commanded us to pray. True prayer is a gift that originates with God, and we are changed when we choose to obey God's command to pray.

---

[9] Calvin. *Institutes*. (3.20.1)

Questions for Reflection

Can you describe a difficult task or situation in which you wanted to quit but kept at it and eventually found it rewarding?

What are your thoughts about prayer being a command given to us by God?

CHAPTER 6
God Always Hears Our Prayers

I travel quite a bit. It's always a blessing meeting new people and hearing their stories, whether I'm on an airplane, getting a ride, or at an event. A question I often ask is, "Can I pray for you?" What's interesting is that I have never had anyone say "no." In fact, most people get teary eyed, say thank you, and act as if no one has ever asked to pray for them. The conversation can get deep pretty quick as people share something that's weighing on them. I've found that most people are dealing with some type of concern. By providing them the opportunity to voice it, God works through those interactions in ways I could have never imagined. Sometimes I pray for them on the spot, and at other times it seems better to pray for them later. When appropriate, I've been able to exchange contact information and follow up later.

Recently, a passenger who had overheard my conversation with the person seated next to me on a plane asked, "Do you really think God hears our prayers?" My answer was a resounding yes! She asked, "How do you know?" To which I replied, "Because God commands us to pray and promises to hear our prayers."

Think about it for a moment. If God did not plan to hear our prayers, then why would he command us to pray? God commands us to pray and provides instructions so we will know how. The problem is that most of us don't like to receive a mandate about anything. When we realize a commandment is for our own good, we can appreciate and enjoy its benefits when we follow it. Parents issue all types of mandates. It doesn't matter if their children get upset about having to look both ways before crossing a street. Out of love and for their safety, the mandate must be issued. Because our heavenly Father knows us better than we will ever know ourselves, which includes knowing what will happen at every moment, God commands us to pray. It is a mandate, and gift, for our own good.

My answer to her first question seemed to suffice, and I am grateful that it prompted the passenger to ask me a second question. "Do you think God needs to hear from us?" What an excellent question! My response was, "No, God doesn't need our prayers, for he is lacking for nothing. He didn't have to create us either but did so out of love and his desire to have relationships with us. As a father, I do not need to hear from my son who is off at college. My day goes on whether I hear from him or not, but I absolutely love to hear from my son every time he calls, regardless of his intentions. How much more our heavenly Father wants to hear from his children!"

Don't just take my word for it. Look at the following passages that reflect God's promise to hear our prayers:

> Come near to God and he will come near to you
> (James 4:8).

> Jesus said, "Ask and it will be given to you; seek and you will find; knock and the door will be opened to you. For everyone who asks receives; the one who seeks finds; and to the one who knocks, the door will be opened" (Luke 11:9-10).

Though some may think it absurd that almighty God would want to hear from lowly creatures, why should we doubt his promise? Famous British minister Charles Spurgeon explains:

When the Creator gives his creature the power of thirst, it is because water exists to meet its thirst. When he creates hunger, there is food to correspond to the appetite. When he inclines men to pray, it is because prayer has a corresponding blessing connected with it. If there is no answer to prayer, prayer is a monstrous absurdity. If it is indeed true that the effects of prayers end with the man who prays, then prayer is a work for idiots and madmen, not for sane people! [10]

Not only does God expect us to pray, he promises to hear every prayer. The reason why we are heard is because of the one who guarantees that we will be heard. Jesus said, "All authority in heaven and on earth has been given to me" (Matthew 28:18). The New Testament also declares that God expects us to pray. Three times in one passage, Jesus said, "When you pray" (Matthew 6:5-7). On another occasion Jesus told his disciples to pray always and not give up (Luke 18:1).

Jesus promises that if we ask, he will listen and respond. Though his response may be different than our request, we can always trust that he will do what is best for his glory and our good. To remind his followers of God's provision, Jesus said, "Consider the ravens: They do not sow or reap, they have no storeroom or barn; yet God feeds them. And how much more valuable you are than birds" (Luke 12:24). Commenting on this passage, Spurgeon said, "Now if God hears a strange, chattering, indistinctive cry as that of a raven, do you not think that he will also hear the rational and expressive prayer of a poor, needy, guilty soul who is crying to him?" Scripture and history reveal that the prayers of believers are always answered:

> If you call out for insight and cry aloud for understanding, and if you look for it as for silver and search for it as for

---

[10] Charles Spurgeon. *The Power in Prayer*. (New Kensington, PA: Whitaker House, 1996), 9-10.

hidden treasure, then you will understand the fear of the Lord and find the knowledge of God (Proverbs 2:3-5).

God does not hear us because of the quality of our effort in prayer, but on the grounds of our redemption through Jesus.[11] Because all authority has been given to Jesus, he is able to hear every prayer. When we choose to pray, we are reminded that Jesus delights in our prayers, which will eventually make our praying become more delightful.

Questions for Reflection

Do you believe that God always hears our prayers? Why or why not?

Can you give an example of a time when God answered a specific prayer?

---

[11] Oswald Chambers. *Prayer: A Holy Occupation*. ed. Harry Verploegh. (Grand Rapids: Oswald Chambers Publications, 1992), 19.

CHAPTER 7
God's Timing and Responses to Our Prayers (Yes, No, Wait)

A kind man who mowed yards in our neighborhood would often stop to ask how our family was doing. Anytime I mentioned the challenges of life or upcoming decisions needed to be made, he would smile and say, "You've got to remember to PUSH! You know, Pray Until Something Happens!" He was right. God wants us to pray until something happens. The "something" may occur externally or within us, but God promises to respond to every prayer. Regardless of where we are in life, God expects us to pray. God also decides when the responses will come.

The testimony of sixteenth-century theologian William Tyndale is a prime example of prayers being answered according to God's timing. Just before being executed as a martyr, Tyndale prayed for the Lord to open the eyes of the King of England so that his translation of the Bible into English from the original Hebrew and Greek languages would be made available for the people of England to read the Bible in their native language.

Two years after Tyndale's death, King Henry VIII declared that every church in England must contain an English translation of the Bible. Unbeknownst to Henry VIII, the English Bible he ordered to be placed in the churches was Tyndale's translation. Tyndale's dying prayer had been answered, bringing the living words of God to the people in a language they could understand. Perhaps just as remarkable is that the English translation of the Bible authorized to be published by King James a century later contained 90% of Tyndale's work. William Tyndale died for his faith, but he did not die in vain. His dying prayer was answered in God's timing.

Like much of life, the outcome of our prayers may be different than what we expect or desire. This being the case, what are we to make of the times when we diligently and sincerely prayed for something and it didn't happen? What about the times when God's response seemed different than what was requested?

It could be that we prayed, even zealously, for the wrong things. I have also discovered that God will sometimes deny what we want in order to give us what we really need. If we were given everything we requested, we would probably be miserable. As a parent, I am not going to give my children everything they want, regardless of how persistently they ask for it. They love candy, and I am happy to provide it for them on occasion; but too much of a delicious thing like candy can eventually cause all sorts of problems, like an upset stomach or cavities. Children, on the other hand, often fail to realize why parents refuse to give them everything they want or when they want it.

Sometimes parents reject the pleas of children because they want to give them something better than what they have asked for. I remember hearing a story about a daughter begging her father to purchase a plastic pearl necklace while waiting in the checkout line at a grocery store. She said, "Daddy, that necklace will make me look like a princess." The father delighted in her asking, but also knew that the necklace was cheap and prone to break. Despite her pleas, the father refused to give his daughter what she wanted, even though she genuinely thought the fake necklace would make her happy. What the child didn't realize or want to hear at the time was that her father had something much better to give her.

Later that evening, the father presented his daughter with a beautiful, authentic pearl necklace that had belonged to her grandmother. "This is for you, my little princess!" The daughter couldn't help but jump for joy and thank her father for giving something better than what she originally wanted. She had been denied what she wanted only to be given something much better. It was worth the wait!

How often do we ask for less than what God wants to give us? Our ideas of what is best, and God's knowledge of what is best, are usually farther apart than the difference between a plastic pearl necklace and an expensive set of genuine pearls (Matthew 13:45-46). Because God only wants what is best for his children, we should not be discouraged when he does not grant a favorable response to prayers that contradict, or are less than, what is best for us. Though material blessings matter, the greatest blessings we can receive through praying are spiritual—the most important being spending time with God.

It has been said that timing is everything. Though our perception of time is limited, God transcends time and will always respond with the big picture in mind. A friend often reminds me that God is never late, but rarely early. Two things are certain: God's timing is perfect, and he always does what is best. During those times when we think God is not listening, he is often working in ways that we can neither see nor understand. The silence might result from us not being ready to receive what God will provide. This may be the case, but it is important to remember that God's silence does not indicate his absence.

In fact, I have discovered that sometimes the Lord remains silent in order to draw us closer or teach patience and trust. After all, is there a better way to learn patience than being forced to wait? The prophet Daniel prayed and waited twenty-one days for God's response (Daniel 10:2-4). The apostle Paul asked the Lord three times to take away the "thorn" that was plaguing him, yet God refused to grant his persistent prayer (2 Corinthians 12:8-10). The most important lessons are often learned during times of waiting.

Sometimes our prayer requests are denied altogether. When this happens, it is important to remember that God, who knows what is best in a way that we do not, may deny what we request in order to give us what we need. Every spring, many high school seniors receive denial letters from college admissions offices. It is interesting how many of us pray for God to make our decisions clear, but when our top choices are eliminated, we don't like it.

Rather than ignoring or dismissing the real feelings of rejection, it is important to allow every student and family the opportunity to work through their disappointment. At some point, however, it is appropriate to thank God for making clear where students will not be attending college. Whether it has to do with college admissions, relationships, or a potential job, we come to realize that every closed door leads to another one opening. The denial is often a blessing in disguise, even though we may not realize or like it at the time. Because God is all-knowing, all-loving, and all-powerful, we can be confident that he will always do what is best in response to our prayers.

Questions for Reflection

What are the three ways in which God responds to prayer?

Can you share an example of a time when God answered a specific prayer, but not when you thought the answer would come?

CHAPTER 8
The Problem of Sin

Jesus was once asked, "What is the most important commandment?" His response was, "Love the Lord your God with all your heart and with all your soul and with all your mind and with all your strength. The second is this: Love your neighbor as yourself" (Mark 12:28-30). This straightforward command may sound easy, but it is really hard to follow on a consistent basis because most of us care more about ourselves than God or others.

We all make mistakes, and sometimes intentionally. Though sin can be described as willful disobedience, the *Westminster Confession of Faith* defines sin as, "Any want of conformity to, or transgression of, any law of God." The Bible states that, "No one is righteous" (Romans 3:10). The word "sin" doesn't sit well with some people, yet everyone has to deal with it. It may be hard to accept the fact that humans are intrinsically bad, but one merely has to spend a couple hours with a group of two-year old children to realize this is true. No one has to teach them to be adorable or mischievous. No one has to teach them to steal a toy or hit the playmate over the head with the stolen toy if they want it back. Using words like "no" and "mine" dominate their vocabulary and remind us why that age group is referred to as the "Terrible Twos."

Most of us learn to behave a little better as life unfolds, but we will never be able to overcome our sinful nature. The reason why is because sin is part of our flawed spiritual DNA. This inherited disease called "original sin" originated in the Garden of Eden (Genesis 3). Let me try to explain it in a more festive way.

Christmas is the most wonderful time of year at our house. For many years we picked out the best Christmas tree, brought it home, and carefully decorated it with all sorts of memorable ornaments that are unique to our family. We all know every Christmas tree is dead, but we enjoy decorating them nonetheless. In a matter of weeks, the results of the tree trunk being cut off from its source of life can no longer be ignored.

Our lives are very similar. Though we build careers and decorate our resumes and offices with an array of achievements for all to see, we are dying from the moment we are born. St. Augustine said it best: "This life is a dying life, no matter what finite comforts it affords us, no matter the companions it brings us, no matter what wealth it lavishes on us."[12] Humans are like every Christmas tree brought home over the years that withered and died. Though we are physically alive, our spiritual nature has been dead from the beginning (Ephesians 2:3).

The Bible states that at birth, we "are dead in our transgressions." This is bad news, which only God can make right. Thankfully, because of God's great love for us, he sent Christ to save us from our misplaced desires and the consequences of sin (Ephesians 2:1-10). The apostle Paul's explanation was that, "While we were powerless, Christ died for the ungodly" (Romans 5:6). He also said, "If anyone is in Christ, the new creation has come: The old has gone, the new is here" (2 Corinthians 5:17). This is what is meant by being "born again." Every person responding in faith to God's unmerited favor (grace) is reconnecting to God as a new creature and will live forever in God's presence (Romans 6). Christians refer to this gracious act of God rescuing his creatures as the "Good News," which is also referred to

---

[12] Quoted in Christopher A. Hall. *Worshiping with the Church Fathers*. (Downers Grove, Illinois: InterVarsity Press, 2009), 144.

as the "gospel." Embracing the Good News reconnects us to God.

Everyone is a creature of God, but not everyone becomes an adopted child of the heavenly Father. Though anyone can be rescued, only those who embrace God's free gift of grace and forgiveness will be saved. The apostle Paul explained the gospel this way: "Because of his great love for us, God, who is rich in mercy, made us alive with Christ even when we were dead in transgressions—it is by grace you have been saved" (Ephesians 2:4-5). The way one enters into a formal relationship with the heavenly Father as a redeemed child is sealed with a prayer. The Bible states, "If you confess with your mouth that Jesus is Lord and believe in your heart that God raised him from the dead, you will be saved" (Romans 10:9). Once a person becomes a Christian, eternal salvation is secure, and the adventure of growing in faith, love, and service to God and others begins.

Perhaps you're still thinking about the Christmas tree analogy. The idea was prompted by Jesus not only dying on a cross made out of a tree, but also his usage of a vine and branches analogy to explain the Good News. Jesus declared, "I am the Vine, you are my branches. If you remain in me, you will bear much fruit" (John 15). We can pretend all is well and ignore the fact that it is not, just like we do with our "live" Christmas trees every year. Eventually, our fruitless lives will become noticeable to all. If we don't pray, we will not be able to do anything that matters in the end. Prayer enables us (the branches) to connect with God (the Vine) in the first place. If we don't stay connected to Christ (the Vine) through prayer, our lives will not be what God desires them to be. This is why Jesus said, "Apart from me you can do nothing," but "if you remain in me, you will bear fruit that lasts" (John 15:5).

Hopefully, one final usage of imagery will drive home the point about living for God. Just as the battery on our phone or computer must be charged in order to be effective, our spiritual batteries must be charged as well. God is the ultimate power source for every believer. Prayer is like the chord that helps believers connect their spiritual batteries into the Holy Spirit's power bank. Unless charged regularly, the battery on the phone or computer will become ineffective. Likewise, we must stay spiritually charged by connecting to God through Bible reading and prayer in order to serve most effectively.

Questions for Reflection

What are some ways that sin separates us from God and prevents us from praying?

How does God use prayer to keep us from sinning, and also produce fruit that lasts?

CHAPTER 9
Prayer and the Seven Deadly Sins

Sin may seem pleasurable for a season, but the negative consequences will surface at some point. Renowned minister, Adrian Rogers, described the consequences of sin in this way:

> Sin will take you farther than you plan to go, make you stay longer than you plan to stay, and before it is done with you, it will make you pay far more than you thought you would pay.[13]

Though others may be unaware of our sin, we cannot hide our sin from God. Realizing God already knows everything we think, say, and do, there is no reason to hold back anything when praying. Just as honest, transparent communication develops trust among people, it also strengthens our relationship with God.

Though temptation is unavoidable, succumbing to it can be avoided. God will always provide a way out (1 Corinthians 10:13). One way to approach the topic is to think about temptation as a door leading to a room full of danger. The door may look attractive and draw us closer to the room, but we always have a choice to walk away from the door of temptation. Knowing that having just one drink

---

[13] Thanks to dear friend Jay Easterling, who sat under Rogers's teaching for many years, for sharing this powerful quote with me.

can lead to detrimental consequences, an alcoholic knows that the way to avoid going into the room of drunkenness is to avoid going near the door of temptation in the first place.

One of the first things an alcoholic has to admit is that they are suffering from the disease of alcoholism. The bottle seemed to work for a while and then it didn't. Bad consequences followed bad choices. Though some deny or genuinely do not realize the depth of their problem, it is still a problem. The choices moving forward are to continue ignoring the problem or get help. In a way similar to a physical illness, sin is a spiritual disease. Like cancer, if ignored or undetected, the consequences can be deadly–both physically and spiritually.

Sin comes in all shapes and sizes. Rather than trying to rate some sins as being less harmful than others, it is important to realize how one sin often leads to more sinning. The Bible mentions that there are seven major sins or abominations (Proverbs 26:24-25). Many great historical figures, such as Thomas Aquinas, addressed the seven "capital" sins, which have also been referred to as the seven "vices" or "deadly" sins. The Gospels in general, and teachings of Jesus in particular, mention the seven capital sins, as well as the corresponding or opposing virtues to each (Matthew 12:43-45; Luke 11:24-26). Below is a chart listing each capital sin (problem) and the opposite virtue (remedy) needed to overcome each one:

The Seven Capital Sins and Opposing Virtues

Pride - Humility
Envy - Mercy
Anger - Meekness
Greed - Generosity
Lust - Chastity
Gluttony - Temperance
Sloth - Diligence

Though everyone struggles with one or more of the capital sins, not everyone is affected in the same way or suffers the same consequences from sinning. Though each person should be aware of the dangers of each of the capital sins, the key is to identify which ones are most tempting, and then learn to cultivate the opposite virtue. Here are a few brief suggestions to consider when dealing with certain capital sins:

Anger - Meekness. A friend of mine has a plaque in her office that reads, "I love Jesus, but I cuss a little." Sometimes it's hard not to cuss when really angry, much less pray, yet the Bible tells us not to sin when angry and "not to let the sun go down on our anger" (Ephesians 4:26). The way to cultivate meekness is to ask God to remove our anger and to trust that God will make things right at the proper time. Though it may not always feel like it, God cares even more about injustice than we do. He will one day address all injustice and restore what was broken and lost. Though we experience loss now, we can be confident that we will not experience ultimate loss (Romans 8:28). Additionally, it is much harder to be angry with the people we are praying for as well.

Greed - Generosity. For the one who struggles with greed, showing generosity is helpful. The Bible reminds us that, "Every good and perfect gift comes from God," therefore we should ask the Lord to help us be generous with the resources he has entrusted to our care (James 1:17). Many people have observed that it is easier to be generous with other people's resources than our own. While that might be a humorous way to put it, it can help us to be generous when we remember that all of our resources do indeed belong to God, not to us.

Gluttony - Temperance. For the one prone to unhealthy eating or drinking habits, learning to show temperance should be the goal. Sometimes total avoidance is the best form of prevention. We can ask the Lord to help us avoid the people or situations that may encourage any form of overindulgence, and also have accountability partners to pray for us.

While spending forty days in the wilderness praying and fasting prior to starting his public ministry, Jesus was tempted by the devil on three occasions. All three times he responded with a passage of scripture. Knowing the areas in which we are most vulnerable and prone to sin is vital to our respective spiritual journey. Memorizing scripture to shield us from those temptations is also essential. It's why the apostle Paul gave these instructions regarding temptation:

> Finally, be strong in the Lord and in his mighty power. Put on the full armor of God, so that you can take your stand against the devil's schemes. For our struggle is not against flesh and blood, but against the rulers, against the authorities, against the powers of this dark world and against the spiritual forces of evil in the heavenly realms. Therefore, put on the full armor of God, so that when the day of evil comes, you may be able to stand your ground, and after you have done everything, to stand (Ephesians 6:10-13).

Prayer and scripture are the best defenses against temptation. However, because our blind spots may be noticeable only to those closest to us, it is really important to have designated accountability partners. These people can check on us and commit to pray for and with us on a regular basis. It is a major reason why churches have small groups and times of confession, why alcoholics go to AA meetings, and why apps have been developed to help those who struggle with on-line addictions. We cannot have enough accountability or prayer in our lives. A friend of mine often says, "Let go, and let God!" Praying is the best way to let God help us overcome our struggles with temptation and sin.

Questions and Actions for Reflection

Can you identify the capital sins that you are most prone to struggle with? Pray for God to help you develop the opposing virtue for each one.

Reflect on Adrian Rogers's comment, "Sin will take you farther than you plan to go, make you stay longer than you plan to stay, and before it is done with you, it will make you pay far more than you thought you would pay." Have you found this to be true in your life? If so, what lesson did you learn?

CHAPTER 10
Confession and Prayer

Repentance is at the heart of confession. Prayer makes confession possible. Apart from Christ and the biblical writers, few have had a greater influence on Christianity than St. Augustine, a fourth century bishop in the northern African city of Hippo. Yet, Augustine was not always a "saint." In fact, prior to his conversion, Augustine pursued everything except God. His autobiography, *Confessions*, is one of the most transparent and encouraging memoirs I have ever read.

Reflecting upon his pre-conversion years, Augustine said, "I looked for pleasure, beauty, and truth not in God, but in myself and his other creatures. That search led me instead to pain, confusion, and error." Because of grace alone, Augustine realized his sin and offered a prayer of praise to his Savior: "You awaken and stir us so that only in praising you can we be content. You have made us for yourself, and our hearts are restless until they find their rest in you."[14]

Catholic priest Thomas Merton also came to Christ after realizing there will always be a battle between one's flesh (sinful nature) and new nature:

---

[14] Augustine. *The Confessions*. (New York: Vintage, 1998), 1.20.

I had fallen asleep in my sweet security. I was living as if God only existed to do me temporal favors. Only when all pride, all self-love has been consumed in our souls by the love of God, are we delivered from the thing which is the subject of those torments. It is only when we have lost all love of ourselves, for our own sakes, that our past sins cease to give us any cause for suffering or for the anguish of shame.[15]

Both Augustine and Merton demonstrated repentance by turning away from their sins and confessing them to God. As promised, God provided forgiveness, salvation, and ability to live in obedience. The ability to acknowledge, confess, and turn away from their sins was only possible because of God. Their testimonies remind us of the importance of confessing sins to God, and others who have been offended (James 5:16).

As a parent, I usually know when my boys have made mistakes, as well as the motive behind their actions. Regardless of their intentions, I am delighted when they come to me with their questions, frustrations, and apologies. I often think about the day when my nine-year-old son yelled at his two-year-old brother for dumping an entire container of fish food into our aquarium. When I arrived on the chaotic scene, fish were darting back and forth, feasting on hundreds of flakes floating on the surface of the water. Our aquarium tank had been transformed into an enormous bowl of fish cereal. Both sons were eager to see if the fish would survive from overindulgence, and thankfully all but one were spared.

As I began lecturing my sons about how all of our fish could have died and how our youngest had no business feeding the fish again, my oldest son, sensing my disappointment and frustration, decided to speak up. "Dad, I'm the one who overfed the fish. Don't

---

[15] Thomas Merton. *The Seven Storey Mountain*. (New York: Harcourt, 1998), 322-323.

get mad at my brother. It was my fault! He had nothing to do with it." The confession made me smile and my oldest son feel better, not to mention letting his younger brother off the hook for being blamed for nearly killing all of our fish. It also brought me joy as a father to watch my son being honest and taking responsibility for his actions. It built trust and strengthened our relationship as well. In a similar yet far more intimate way, our heavenly Father desires to hear from us, and will forgive all who confess their sins (Matthew 7:11; Romans 10:9).

Honesty is the essence of confession. When we are honest before God, who is perfect and holy in every way, we realize our sinful nature and how much we need his grace. I am reminded of the time I went shopping for a diamond ring. Diamonds are radiant. Every jeweler knows that placing diamonds against a piece of dark colored velvet makes them dazzle even more. However, if you look very closely, especially with a magnifying glass, you will notice small blemishes within most diamonds that are undetectable otherwise.

The more we focus on the holy God who is perfect in every way, the more we notice the blemishes in our lives that need to be removed. King David messed up badly on multiple occasions, including committing adultery and murder. Psalm 51 is his prayer of confession. Notice the first two verses:

> Have mercy upon me, O God,
>   according to your loving kindness;
>   according to the multitude of your tender mercies,
>   blot out my transgressions.
> Wash me thoroughly from my iniquity,
>   and cleanse me from my sin.

Later in this psalm, David said, "Create in me a clean heart, O Lord. And renew a steadfast spirit within me" (vs. 10).

Prayerful

True repentance requires words and actions. Anyone can apologize with words, but when actions and words of confession align, one can experience true forgiveness. Recognizing sin is imperative; so is confessing our sins to God. If our sins seem too great to confess, we need to remember that God's grace is always greater than our sins. King David knew the importance of asking God for conviction of sin and to renew a steadfast spirit within him. We can do the same through prayer.

Most of us don't like to admit being wrong or needing to confess anything–which is why it is important to allow close friends to ask tough questions and pray for us on a daily basis. One cannot have enough accountability. John Wesley, founder of the Methodist Church, encouraged small groups to ask important questions of themselves and others each day. The most piercing question was, "How have you sinned today?" It is a question most of us don't want to hear, but not thinking about it only enables us to ignore what is obvious to God, and sometimes others, about our lives.

Each of us is a sinner who falls short of God's standard every day (Romans 3:23). The consequences of our sin strains relationships with God and others, which is why we need to confess our sins every day. One thing I have found helpful is to ask God to reveal to me at the end of the day when I messed up with my words and actions throughout the day. Without fail, God reveals to me something I need to confess.

Millions of Christians who follow the *Book of Common Prayer* or other Daily Office pray the following, or similar, Prayer of Confession on a daily basis. You may choose to use it as a guide to your time of confession as well.

> Most merciful God,
> we confess that we have sinned against you
> in thought, word, and deed,

by what we have done,
and by what we have left undone.
We have not loved you with our whole heart;
we have not loved our neighbors as ourselves.
We are truly sorry and we humbly repent.
For the sake of your Son Jesus Christ,
have mercy on us and forgive us;
that we may delight in your will,
and walk in your ways,
to the glory of your name, Amen.

When a tax collector realized his transgressions, he confessed to God: "God, have mercy on me, a sinner"(Luke 18:13). Today, we can pray: "Lord Jesus Christ, Son of God, have mercy on me, a sinner." This simple prayer is often referred to as the "Jesus Prayer." Within the Greek Orthodox Church, it has been abbreviated to simply, "Lord, have mercy."

Psalm 103:12 states, "As far as the east is from the west, God has forgiven our sins." We are already forgiven; when we confess our sins through prayer, we will receive the peace that comes only from the Lord.

Prayerful

Questions for Reflection

St. Augustine wrote to God, "You have made us for yourself, and our hearts are restless until they find their rest in you." What are your thoughts about his confession?

How often do you confess your sins? Every day, perhaps several times per day, consider praying, "Lord Jesus, Son of God, have mercy on me, a sinner." You can also simply pray, "Lord, have mercy."

CHAPTER 11
Praying for Wisdom and Discernment

Though we may be sincere about what we think God intends for us to know and do, we can be sincerely wrong. I am usually skeptical when I hear someone say, "God said to me," or "the Lord wants me to do this or that." It is not that I don't believe them as much as I know from experience that too many of us have desires that differ from God's plans for our lives. What appears good and right may not be what is best for us, which was the case with the first humans in the Garden of Eden. If Adam and Eve had adhered to God's words instead of words that contradicted his instructions, they would have been spared much hardship (and we would have as well).

The same temptations apply to us; therefore when God appears to be speaking, we should make sure what we are "hearing" aligns with the scriptures. What we hear from others should be supported by scripture as well. This matters greatly because even those with the best intentions can mislead us. Not praying for discernment makes us vulnerable to deception. There is also an Enemy that twists the truth to deceive us, just as he did in the Garden of Eden. It is the reason why the best lies contain kernels of truth, and the devil is called the "father of lies" (John 8:44). Thankfully, God has given us the Bible to discern truth from lies. It is one of the main reasons why we need to be familiar with the scriptures, for God's words will never lead us astray. An important passage to remember regarding discernment says:

> Dear friends, do not believe every spirit, but test the spirits to see whether they are from God, because many false prophets have gone out into the world. This is how you can recognize the Spirit of God: Every spirit that acknowledges that Jesus Christ has come in the flesh is from God, but every spirit that does not acknowledge Jesus is not from God. This is the spirit of the antichrist, which you have heard is coming and even now is already in the world (1 John 4:1-3).

If the choices before us contradict the Ten Commandments, the Golden Rule of loving God supremely and others as ourselves, or the abundance of other wisdom and instruction the Bible provides, then we should refrain from those choices. It's one thing to know the scriptures and another to follow its instructions, which is why the Bible says, "Do not merely listen to the word, and so deceive yourselves. Do what it says. Anyone who listens to the word but does not do what it says is like someone who looks at his face in a mirror and, after looking at himself, goes away and immediately forgets what he looks like" (James 1:22-24).

We all need wisdom, and the Bible reminds us that if we ask God for wisdom, it will be provided (James 1:5). It also instructs us not to lean on our understanding, but to acknowledge God in all our ways so that he can guide us in the right direction (Proverbs 3:5-6). Though these passages are straightforward, God's will for our lives can be hard to discern. In addition to using the Bible to help us discern God's will for our daily lives, praying about decisions, no matter how big or small, should also be a top priority. Seeking advice from prayerful people who know us well and desire God's best for us should also play an important role in our decision-making process.

It has been said that the way to hear God laugh is to tell him your plans. This doesn't mean that we should not make plans, for failing to plan can be viewed as planning to fail. We should also share thoughts and plans with others who will listen, pray, and offer advice about what may be best for us. A few days before my senior year in college, a minister asked me what I was planning to do after graduation. After listening quietly to my monologue, he asked, "Have you let God in on your plans?" Sadly, I had not. Instead, I had been too consumed with trying to please others and doing things in my own strength, not to mention thinking I was in control of my future. I had been making decisions without seriously praying about them. It was as if I had been conjuring up plans and then expecting God to bless them. Consequently, when things didn't go my way, I was often left doubting God and myself.

As I have learned to pray about plans, specifically for discernment and direction, God has continuously given me peace and confidence along the way. Another bit of helpful advice regarding how to plan for the future came through reading *The Purpose Driven Life*. The first sentence of that book— "It's not about you!"—has crossed my mind daily for the past twenty years. Ultimately, life is not about me or you. This runs counter to popular marketing slogans seen and heard on a daily basis, such as "You Rule," and "Obey Your Thirst!" Embracing these self-gratifying mantras can satisfy temporary cravings, but adopting them as mission statements for life simply will not work.

If life is not ultimately about us, then what's it all about? It is a question every generation has contemplated. *The Westminster Confession of Faith* states that, "The chief end of man is to glorify God and enjoy him forever." The apostle Paul said, "So whether you eat, drink, or whatever you do, do it all for the glory of God" (1 Corinthians 10:31). This means that we should focus more on following God's plan than our own.

A question I hear frequently from students is, "How can I know what God wants me to do with my life?" Thankfully, God has given us the scriptures and prayer as the means to help us guide our decisions. When the prophet Jeremiah needed direction in life, God provided both a promise and way to receive it:

> For I know the plans I have for you, declares the Lord. Plans for welfare and not for evil, to give you a future and a hope. Then you will call upon me and come and pray to me, and I will hear you. You will seek me and find me, when you seek me with all your heart (Jeremiah 29:11-13 ESV).

Did you notice the condition given to Jeremiah about how to know God's plan for his life? The Lord said, "You will seek me and find me when you seek me with all your heart." Not with some of your energy, schedule, and decisions, but with *all* your heart. Notice how another place in the Bible mentions seeking God with *all* your heart. "Trust in the Lord with all your heart, and do not lean on your own understanding. In all your ways acknowledge God and he will make your paths straight" (Proverbs 3:5-6).

Does this sound familiar? Jesus said, "Seek first my kingdom and righteousness and all these things will be given to you as well" (Matthew 6:33). He also said, "Store up for yourselves treasures in heaven (Matthew 6:20). This means that we should work to build God's eternal kingdom instead of earthly empires that will one day cease to exist. We must also remember that God's plan is better than ours, and that he loves us more than we can ever love ourselves. Reading the Bible and communicating with God through prayer remind us of his promises, love, and grace. Doing so also helps us make better decisions.

Questions for Reflection

How does God help us make wise decisions?

Jesus said, "Seek first my kingdom and righteousness and all these things will be added unto you." He also said, "Store up for yourselves treasures in heaven." What would obeying those passages look like in your life?

CHAPTER 12
Praying with Right Motives

I have never heard a person say, "My prayer life is perfect!" In fact, I don't know anyone who doesn't struggle with prayer being a consistent part of their life. Even those who believe in the power of prayer sometimes pray with wrong intentions. There have been times in life when God seemed distant and few things seemed to go my way. I was often impatient, fretful, irritable, and tired. As I reflect on those negative periods of life, a common theme existed every time – I was either praying with selfish motives or not praying at all. During the time period when Jesus walked the earth, many of his followers had similar struggles. It's the reason St. James said, "You do not have because you do not ask God. When you ask, you do not receive because you ask with wrong motives" (James 4:2-3).

I am assuming you have experienced someone communicating with you only because they wanted something. It's like someone showing up at Christmas to receive gifts without caring anything about the one giving the presents. If someone only speaks to a friend when they want something, that relationship won't be healthy or last very long. It should be no different with our relationship with the Lord. Do you think God fails to realize our motives? We should not value anything above God, even the gifts he can provide (Matthew 6:33). Prayer should be so much more than asking God for the things we need and want. The best part of praying is spending time with God.

Generations of Christians have prayed with ulterior motives, and the Bible provides numerous examples about how not to pray. Jesus said:

> When you pray, do not be like the hypocrites, for they love to pray standing in the synagogues and on the street corners to be seen by men. I tell you the truth, they have received their reward in full. But when you pray, go into your room, close the door and pray to your Father, who is unseen. Then your Father, who sees what is done in secret, will reward you. And when you pray, do not keep on babbling like pagans, for they think they will be heard because of their many words (Matthew 6:5-8).

Several things can be inferred from this passage. Praying with wrong motives is not a good idea, for God knows our true intentions and isn't impressed by lofty prayers. If our motive is to impress others with our prayers, the only thing that might be received by such misplaced intentions will be the applause of others. Because we all are susceptible to becoming distracted and praying with mixed motives, Jesus implores us to be intentional about spending time praying alone. Developing a healthy relationship with God through private prayer was modeled by Christ. Following his example helps prepare us for our public time of prayer as well.

We are free to ask honestly and fully for what we need and want, but the most important request should be for God's will to be done in and through our lives. Oftentimes we get this backwards. How often do we pray only for physical healing while completely ignoring the fact that spiritual healing is far more important? How often do we pray for nonbelievers so that they will be more pleasant to be around instead of praying for their salvation and spiritual growth? At times we've made prayer much more about ourselves and gifts we may receive, rather than praying simply to spend time with the Giver of all good things.

One of the many #1 hits by the famous rock band, *The Rolling Stones*, is called, "You Can't Always Get What You Want." The title and chorus of the song applies to our prayer lives as well, for we will not always get what we want when it comes to prayer. That's a good thing, for imagine how different, and likely worse, our lives would be if God gave us everything we wanted. There is a particular passage of scripture attributed to Jesus that is often taken out of context, even by religious leaders, in order to convince people that God will grant whatever is asked of him:

> If you abide in me, and my words abide in you, ask whatever you wish, and it will be done for you. By this my Father is glorified, that you bear much fruit and so prove to be my disciples. As the Father has loved me, so have I loved you. Abide in my love. If you obey my commandments, you will abide in my love, just as I have kept my Father's commandments and abide in his love (John 15:7-10, ESV).

There are two main conditions tied to Christ's promise to grant "whatever we wish":

1. "If" we abide in Christ and his words abide in us.
2. "If" we keep the commandments and so abide in God's love.

This means that when we properly understand and apply the scriptures to our lives, we will do a better job of keeping God's commandments. It also means that we will abide in Christ's love and bear much fruit as faithful disciples. Living in such obedience causes our prayers to focus solely on God's will to be done. In response, God's answers will correspond with our petitions, oftentimes exceeding our expectations. This is why the apostle Paul exclaimed:

> Now to him who is able to do immeasurably more than all we ask or imagine, according to his power that is at work within us, to him be glory in the church and in Christ Jesus throughout all generations, forever and ever! Amen (Ephesians 3:20).

When our prayers align with God's plans, we can expect him to grant whatever we ask of him as well. Though sometimes difficult, we must always pray for God's glory and will to be done. When we pray in this manner, God's faithfulness will be proven time and time again.

It is also important to point out that there will be times when we have the right intentions, but our actions based on a limited perspective may not align with God's intentions. I have no doubt that God appreciates prayers and service offered with the right intentions, even if our efforts seem fruitless or counterproductive. Recently, my friend Jon shared a story that drives home the point. As a boy, Jon really enjoyed going with his father to fill up the truck with gas, especially knowing he would receive a candy bar every time they paid for the fuel. One particular morning, Jon overheard his father asking his mother if he could drive her car to work because his truck was low on gas. She said, "Sure, Honey, and you can fill up your truck when you get home from work."

Jon, being the creative and helpful boy that he was, decided to save his dad some time and money by filling up the truck around the time his dad would return home from work. While his mother was preparing dinner, Jon went outside and stretched the water hose over to the gas tank on his dad's truck. He had seen his dad do it many times at the gas station. A smile came across Jon's face as he turned on the hose and filled up the gas tank with water. Because there was no automatic sensor to keep the tank from overflowing, before long a mixture of gas and water gushed everywhere. Thankfully,

Jon's father arrived home as he was turning off the water hose. As his dad got out of the car and surveyed the scene, Jon exclaimed, "I filled up your truck, Papa!"

Though he realized the terrible mistake his son had made, Jon's dad, rather than getting angry, simply smiled and said, "thanks for trying to help, Son." Knowing his son's intentions, Jon's father could only laugh and start thinking about how to fix the problem. I have no doubt that our heavenly Father smiles at our limited knowledge, ignorant prayers, and feeble attempts to do his work. Motive matters, and if our desire is to please the Father, he will be pleased with us.

Questions for Reflection

What motivates you to pray?

Do you typically focus more on spending time with God or what you hope to receive through praying?

CHAPTER 13
Humility and Prayer

Humility is also an important component of successful prayer, for the very act of praying demonstrates humility. Choosing to pray is the admission of a need, which is why some people refuse to pray. It's like the guy who won't ask for help because he wants to figure things out on his own. I can't count the number of times I have driven in the wrong direction only to discover I was lost and needed to turn around. I could have saved a lot of time and money if I had learned to ask for directions sooner rather than later. Pride has prevented me from asking for directions and from praying as well.

The opposite of humility is pride, and if we think we are not prideful, we might need a dose of humility. The scriptures talk much about the importance of humility because pride has always been a problem. Jesus began his Sermon on the Mount by exhorting his followers to be humble because pride was preventing them from repenting before God and loving others (Matthew 5). Prideful people not only refuse to ask for help, they usually do not sense the need to ask for forgiveness.

We are all prideful people at times. Spiritual pride and competitiveness can occur even among clergy and congregations. Reflecting on the danger of pride that often follows success, Charles Spurgeon said, "If you can be great without prayer, your greatness will be your ruin. If God means to bless you greatly, he will make you pray greatly."[16] Pride has been the downfall of many influential leaders. In most cases, the leaders lacked the accountability needed to keep their pride in check. It can happen to anyone.

How would you respond to the question, "who is the most prideful person you know?" Very few people would mention themselves or another Christian. Why? Because our tendency is to think of ourselves more highly than we should. It has been said that pride is the root of all evil, and that many sins stem from it. Pride can hinder praying as well. Sixth century monk St. Benedict of Nursia clearly understood the importance of humility and prayer:

> If we want to ask a favor of any person of power, we presume not to approach but with humility and respect. How much more ought we to address ourselves to the Lord and God of all things with a humble and entire devotion?[17]

I remember not wanting to pray aloud in front of others because I cared too much about what people would think about my prayers. I also recall times in life when I refused to pray because I was ungrateful or didn't think I needed God's help. In both cases, pride was the main obstacle I needed to overcome.

Praying with humility has characterized godly persons throughout history. Puritan William Secker stated that, "Pride is the sinner's torment, but humility is a saint's ornament."[18] Another Puritan, Thomas Brooks, wrote:

---

[16] Charles Spurgeon. *Praying Successfully*. (New Kensington, PA: Whitaker House, 1997), 25.

[17] Quoted in B. Jeffrey Bingham, *Pocket History of the Church*. (Downers Grove, IL: InterVarsity Press, 2002), 59.

[18] Quoted in I.D.E. Thomas. *A Puritan Golden Treasury*, (Carlisle, PN: Banner of Truth Trust, 2000), 147.

> God looks not at the elegancy of your prayers, to see how neat they are; nor at the geometry of your prayers to see how long they are; nor at the arithmetic of your prayers to see how many they are; nor at the music of your prayers, nor at the sweetness of your voice, nor at the logic of your prayers; but at the sincerity of your prayers. [19]

Even though some people may be impressed by our prayers, God never will be. I've often been reminded of this truth when listening to the simple prayers of children, as they freely share with God whatever comes to mind. During a bedtime prayer one evening my five-year-old blurted out, "God, why did you make rattlesnakes?" I'm certain God appreciated his honest question.

Not only have I been guilty of trying to impress people with my prayers, but I have also tried to impress people by trying to serve in my own strength instead of relying on God. There have been other times when I was so busy trying to serve the Lord that I failed to utilize God's strength that was needed to serve. In each instance, my pride was the root of the problem.

I've often wondered about how pride has hindered my spiritual journey, especially those instances when I needed help but refused to ask God or others for assistance. It reminds me of the time I watched my four-year-old create a racetrack in a sandbox, only to experience frustration due to a large rock preventing smooth passage for his little cars. I offered to help, but he refused. After ten minutes of digging, kicking, and trying to remove the rock, my son's lip quivered as he started to cry. He then said, "Daddy, I'm so mad about this rock messing up my racetrack, and I can't move it." I then said, "Son, have you thought about asking me for help?" He said, "No, because I didn't think I needed it."

---

[19] Ibid, 212.

Prayerful

It's one thing to watch a determined child persistently trying to accomplish an impossible feat to no avail, and quite another to observe a stubborn adult refusing God's assistance. It was a joy to remove the rock and watch my son's frustration go away that day. In a similar way, God is always nearby, knows exactly what we need, and wants to help. The Bible makes clear that God will give grace to those who are humble, and that when we draw near to God through prayer, he will draw closer to us (James 4:6-8). Asking for assistance demonstrates humility and trust in God's provision, not to mention making life much more enjoyable.

Questions for Reflection

Has there been a time when refusing assistance led to negative consequences in your life? What did you learn from that situation?

What are some things you can do to cultivate humility in your life, particularly as it relates to prayer?

CHAPTER 14
Praying with Thanksgiving

The Bible states that every good and perfect gift comes from God (James 1:17). Because both the desire and ability to pray are gifts from God, we should always give thanks when we pray. I know it can be easier said than done. Despite dealing with many hardships, the apostle Paul declared, "Be joyful always; pray continually; give *thanks* in all circumstances, for this is God's will for you in Jesus Christ" (1 Thessalonians 5:16-18).

Unfortunately, we fail to obey this command when we allow circumstances to dictate our prayer life. Though scripture tells us to pray continually, many times we turn to prayer as a last resort after we have exhausted all other means to remedy our problems. There are times when we would rather bring our concerns to others instead of God. It's as if we have forgotten that God has provided the gift of prayer as a means to give us peace and joy.

To be frank, sometimes I fail to pray because I am ungrateful. Maybe you can relate? If so, consider asking yourself these questions each day: "When was the last time I thanked God for anything besides a meal?" "Is there someone I should thank today?" Sometimes a busy schedule is to blame. Regardless of the reasons for being ungrateful, reading the scriptures often puts things into perspective. Reflect on the following charge written by the apostle Paul while he was confined to a dingy prison cell:

> Rejoice in the Lord always. I will say it again: Rejoice! Let your gentleness be evident to all. The Lord is near. Do not be anxious about anything, but in everything, by prayer and petition, with *thanksgiving*, present your requests to God. And the peace of God, which transcends all understanding, will guard your hearts and your minds in Christ Jesus (Philippians 4:4-7).

God is honored in the manner due him when he is acknowledged as the author of all blessings.[20] Every day is a gift, and every prayer should reflect our thanksgiving to God for all he has provided each day (food, shelter, health, clothing, friends, family, and many more blessings). Because God is the giver of all good things, praying demonstrates both our thanksgiving for and reliance upon God's provision (James 1:17). Because the unfortunate tendency of our culture, typically promoted through various forms of media, is to highlight negative and polarizing things, being intentional about praising and thanking God should be a top priority. I have found that expressing gratitude to God, sometimes through writing down all I am thankful for, makes me more grateful toward others as well.

Who doesn't like an attitude of gratitude? It doesn't take much effort, and God knows our world needs more people to express thanksgiving. My friend Herren gives thanks to God all the time. Not long into most of our conversations, he'll say, "Thank you, Lord, for this day and the many blessings you've given us." His occasional mini prayers woven into our chats remind me that God is truly part of our three-way conversations. His sincere gratitude is contagious and impacts everyone around him.

When was the last time you said, "Thank you?" Thirteenth century German theologian Meister Eckhart once said, "If the only prayer you ever say in your entire life is thank you, it will be enough." It seems

---

[20] John Calvin, *Institutes* (3.20.28).

that my friend has adopted this mentality for every conversation. I have witnessed on numerous occasions how Herren's demonstration of genuine gratitude makes everyone feel special. From complimenting a hostess or waiter at a restaurant, to thanking a clerk at a store, for what I have considered people merely doing their jobs, Herren always strives to encourage people with kindness and gratitude. May God help us to pray and serve with thanksgiving as well. Sometimes simply saying thank you will be enough.

Questions for Reflection

What are you thankful for? Consider all that you have been given and then offer a prayer of thanksgiving to God. Consider writing down your prayers of thanksgiving as well. Try it, and you will discover how encouraging this practice can be.

If you could have tomorrow only what you gave thanks to God for today, what might you have left?

CHAPTER 15
Praying Through Trials

Difficult circumstances often help us realize our need for God. Not only does God discipline those he loves, he also uses trials to get our undivided attention (Hebrews 12:6-8). For some people, nothing else would enable them to realize their desperate need for God and prayer. Because this world is not our home, we should not expect life to be predictable or easy.

Daily headlines remind us that things are not as they should be. Sometimes trouble results from poor choices, but trials can also occur without explanation. It seems that if one has not recently experienced a trial, the next challenge is somewhere on the horizon. No one is exempt, for even those living in obedience to God will face adversity along the way (Romans 8:17; 2 Timothy 3:12).

Thankfully, because there is never a moment when we are not in the presence of God, we do not have to face trials alone. Notice how the psalmist describes God's intimate awareness of our lives:

> O Lord, you have searched me and you know me. You know when I sit and when I rise; you perceive my thoughts from afar. You discern my going out and my lying down; you are familiar with all my ways. Before a word is on my tongue you know it completely, O Lord…Where can I go from your Spirit? Where can I flee from your presence?

> Your eyes saw my unformed body; All the days ordained for me were written in your book before one of them came to be. How precious to me are your thoughts, O God (Psalm 139:1-4, 7, 16-17).

This beautiful psalm is a reminder that you and I are in the thoughts of God. It also reminds us that God knows every detail of our lives. This means that delays, accidents, and even tragedies, can be used by God for purposes we simply cannot understand this side of eternity. Though our circumstances may not make sense to us, God knows and cares about everything we encounter.

Because we live in a fallen, broken world, life will be challenging. It's always been this way. Those truly living for God are guaranteed opposition at some point. The apostle Peter reminded the earliest believers of this reality:

> Dear friends, do not be surprised at the painful trial you are suffering, as though something strange were happening to you. But rejoice that you participate in the sufferings of Christ, so that you may be overjoyed when his glory is revealed. If you are insulted because of the name of Christ, you are blessed, for the Spirit of glory and of God rests on you (1 Peter 4:12-14).

James, who led the church in Jerusalem and was also martyred for his faith, made a similar proclamation:

> Consider it pure joy, my brothers, whenever you face trials of many kinds, because you know that the testing of your faith develops perseverance. Perseverance must finish its work so that you may be mature and complete, not lacking anything (James 1:2-4).

James and Peter are saying the same thing—that challenges will come, and faith is proven genuine during trials (1 Peter 1:6-7). There is no better example of this reality than the death of Jesus.

No one except Jesus seemed to understand the victory that would come after his death on the cross. In the immediate aftermath of Christ's death, his closest followers scattered in confusion and fear. Even Peter denied Jesus on three occasions. Thankfully, Jesus understood and forgave his failings, just as he puts up with our failures and lack of understanding.

It is hard to remember these truths when going through a trial because we are usually preoccupied with doubts, fear, and wondering when the trial will end. The apostle Paul, when plagued by a burden, asked God multiple times to take it away. Make note of God's response to Paul's specific request to remove his trial: "My grace is sufficient for you, for my power is made perfect in weakness" (2 Corinthians 12:7-9). God's response to Paul does not mean that we should refrain from sharing our frustrations and pain with God. Rather, like Paul, we should realize that trials can bring us closer to God when we pray. Because God desires intimacy with us, it is possible that trials may be used to strengthen our prayer life.

I know that when things seem to be going well, I tend to pray less, but during challenging times I often pray more. In fact, my most fervent prayers have occurred during trials. Trials have a way of reminding us that we are just as dependent on God during times of smooth sailing as when the storms of life rock our boats. Amid the storms, I have often asked God, "Why are you allowing this to happen to me?" Though an appropriate question, I've found it more useful to ask God, "What is it that you want to teach me through my circumstances?"

Though scripture describes Jesus literally calming a storm and walking on rough waves, it also reveals instances when Christ allowed trials to linger for his greater purposes, like when he waited several days before raising his friend Lazarus from the dead (John 11:38-

44). Though we may never understand the reason for trials, several truths should be embraced when facing them: God is with us. God loves us. God is in control. God always does what is best, even if it doesn't seem like it at the time. Though God may allow stormy circumstances to persist, he can calm the storms in our minds if we turn to him in prayer (Isaiah 26:3).

Something else to keep in mind when life doesn't make sense is that God's ways are not our ways, and his thoughts are not our thoughts (Isaiah 55:8-9). Though no one wants to experience trials, I have had numerous people tell me that nothing else would have grabbed their attention. Though life can be hard and seem unfair, the key is to communicate with God through prayer. After all, the Bible tells us that, "If we cast our burdens on the Lord, he will sustain us" (Psalm 55:22). This means that trials can be viewed as invitations to pray. Our persistence in prayer shows both our confidence that God is our only hope, and our belief that he will act in the best way and time in response to our persistent pleas.[21]

Though many metaphors are used in the scriptures to describe God, one of the most helpful as it relates to trials is found in the Book of Malachi. Malachi describes God as a refiner and purifier of silver and gold (Malachi 3). Just as the silversmith uses fire to purify precious metals, God as the master Silversmith can use fiery trials to purify us of sin. Just as the silversmith uses a hammer to pound the metal into the shape he desires, trials can be viewed as God's necessary means by which to form us into the image of Christ. Though we may feel forsaken, just as Jesus felt while dying on the cross, the heavenly Father is with us at every moment as well. When Jesus knew the trial was complete, he declared from the cross, "It is finished" (John 19:30). As a silversmith knows his masterpiece is nearing completion, he looks more intently at the art he is creating.

---

[21] John Piper. *What Jesus Demands from the World*. (Wheaton, IL: Crossway, 2006), 108.

The way he knows it is finished is when he sees his reflection in it! One day God will see his perfect image in us and declare again, "It is finished!"

Jesus never once told his disciples that obedience would prevent them from suffering. In fact, Jesus told them, "In this world you will have trouble, but take heart! I have overcome the world" (John 16:33). Christ's victory enables us to overcome trials as well.

Questions for Reflection

Have you ever experienced a trial that resulted in a good outcome that could have never happened otherwise?

It has been said that our faith is proven genuine during trials. How has this been true in your life or in the life of someone you know?

CHAPTER 16
Turning Worry into Prayer

Webster's dictionary defines worry as "uneasiness of mind, usually over an impending or anticipated event."[22] Not only does everyone worry, but most people worry about things that never happen. A research study conducted by Penn State University revealed that 91% of things people worry about never happen, and of the 9% that come to fruition, the outcome is far better than anticipated. For one in four participants in the study, none of their worries materialized.[23]

Perhaps you are worried about something right now. Finding a job, making enough money, trying to please others, dealing with health concerns, deciding which college to attend, whom to date or marry, the constant threat of terrorism, or dealing with another world war are things that cause anxiety for many people. A recent Gallup research poll revealed that 51% of college students worry on a daily basis.[24] Statistics can be helpful, but it doesn't take a survey to know that people of all ages are worried about something.

How does one know when worry has become a problem? It certainly affects different people in different ways. Intense worry is

---

[22] www.merriam-webster.com

[23] www.psychologytoday.com

[24] www.gallup.com

usually accompanied by sweat, tension, an increased pulse, trouble sleeping, difficulty concentrating, dry mouth, or digestive issues. Not only do symptoms vary, but so do the ways in which different people respond to anxiety. I wish overcoming stress was as easy as singing the chorus of a number one hit from many years ago–"Don't worry, be happy. Don't worry, be happy now!"

Listening to music or singing a favorite song can certainly be therapeutic, but many people choose methods that can make matters worse. The consumption of alcohol or drugs has become all too common. Despite health warnings, one of my relatives started smoking at age forty to cope with the stress that came with a new job. A friend during college chose to stuff himself with food each time he got stressed out. Abusing alcohol and food isn't good, but some people do so anyway.

Because worry is an inevitable part of life, the key is to learn how to identify catalysts that cause you to worry, and then develop a plan to deal with it. Sharing concerns with people who care about you is a good place to start. Seeking pastoral and professional help is necessary for some people. Exercise, sufficient sleep, and a healthy diet can also help remedy the problem.

Anxiety has been a problem for every generation, including those who lived when Jesus walked the earth. Below are several biblical passages that are as relevant today as when written during the first century.

Jesus once said to his followers:

> Therefore, I tell you, do not worry about your life, what you will eat or drink, or about your body, what you will wear. Is not life more important than food, and the body more important than clothes? Look at the birds of the air; they do not sow or reap or store away in barns, and yet your heavenly Father feeds them. Are you not much more valuable than

they? Who of you by worrying can add a single hour to his life? And why do you worry about clothes? See how the lilies of the field grow. They do not labor or spin. Yet I tell you that not even Solomon in all his splendor was dressed like one of these. If that is how God clothes the grass of the field, which is here today and tomorrow is thrown into the fire, will he not much more clothe you, O you of little faith? So do not worry, saying, "What shall we eat? Or What shall we drink? Or what shall we wear?" For the pagans run after all these things, and your heavenly Father knows that you need them. But seek first his kingdom and his righteousness, and all these things will be given to you as well. Therefore, do not worry about tomorrow, for tomorrow will worry about itself. Each day has enough trouble of its own (Matthew 6:25-34).

Reading scripture reminds us of God's character and promises, which in turn helps us to realize that he is bigger than our worry and can help us be less anxious.

Notice what the apostle Paul wrote from a prison cell to believers living in the Greek city of Philippi:

> Do not be anxious about anything, but in everything, by prayer and petition, with thanksgiving, present your requests to God. And the peace of God, which transcends all understanding, will guard your hearts and your minds in Christ Jesus (Philippians 4:6-7).

Paul could have chosen to live his remaining days worrying, as if the promises and victory of Christ were not true. Instead, he chose to trust his future to the one who had already been through everything he could ever face. It is why Paul exclaimed, "For me to live is Christ, and to die is gain" (Philippians 1:21). In what would be his last letter written from prison before his execution, Paul shared advice with a young student named Timothy that is just as applicable to modern readers:

> God gave us a spirit not of fear, but of power and love and self-control (2 Timothy 1:7, ESV).

Paul's letter echoes much of what was written in the psalter centuries earlier:

> God heals the brokenhearted and binds up their wounds. He determines the number of the stars and calls them each by name. Great is our Lord and mighty in power; his understanding has no limit (Psalm 147:3-5).

Hebrews 13:8 states, "Jesus is the same yesterday, today, and forever." Because God never changes and is in complete control, we really do not need to worry. I know it is easier said than done, especially for the one struggling. There were times during college when I worried about my grades, work, relationships, faith, and future. I'll never forget a mentor's advice that helped me overcome my fears: "Having concern about life is not the same as worrying about life. Life has its challenges, but you need to realize that worrying is a choice."

As we continued the conversation, I realized that the issue was not that I worried, but what I did with my worry. As we read the words of Jesus recorded in the Gospel of Matthew above, worry doesn't change or solve anything (Matthew 6:27). The personal breakthrough came when I chose to turn my worry into prayer. Each time I worried, I decided to pray and read the Bible. Two helpful passages for reflection are:

> You keep in perfect peace whose mind is stayed on you (Isaiah 26:3, ESV).

Cast your cares on the Lord and he will sustain you; he will never let the righteous fall (Psalm 55:22).

As I learned to share my burdens with the Lord instead of always feeling the need to go to others first or trying to solve problems in my own strength, a couple of positive things happened. As time went on, I found myself praying more and worrying less. I also drew closer to God. Life has its challenges, but through prayer and scripture reading, God can replace our worry with peace and power.

Questions for Reflection

Given what has been discussed in this chapter, what advice can you apply to your own life, or share with others struggling with worry?

What are the most prevalent things causing anxiety in your life right now? Make a list and ask God to take away your worry and fears and replace them with peace and hope.

CHAPTER 17
Meditating on and Praying Scripture (Lectio Divina)

Your prayer life will often be a reflection of your view of and trust in God. The better your knowledge of God, the more intimate and powerful your prayers will be.[25] Because we come to know God best through the scriptures, the most fruitful prayers are rooted in the scriptures. There are no better words to guide our thoughts and prayers than the very words of God. Like a map designed to guide us to a destination, the Bible can be viewed as God's map for our lives. Simply put, if we don't read the map, how can we arrive at the destination God desires for our lives?

Though important resources containing scripture exist to encourage prayer, like the *Book of Common Prayer*, this book and other secondary sources, none will ever be on par with the divinely inspired words of scripture. The truth is, none of us read the Bible as we should, which in turn causes us to focus more on temporary things rather than eternal treasures. Pope Gregory the Great, in a letter written to the emperor's physician, explains:

---

[25] Timothy Keller. *Prayer: Experiencing Awe and Intimacy with God*. (New York: Dutton, 2014), 49.

Prayerful

> The king of heaven, the Lord of men and angels, has written you a letter that you may live, and yet, illustrious son, you neglect to read it with ardent love. Strive therefore, I beg you, to meditate each day on the words of your Creator. Learn to know the heart of God in the words of God. Thus, you will long for the things of heaven with greater desire, and your soul will be more eager for the joys that are invisible.[26]

When you read the Bible, you encounter God's living words–which is why Gregory begged his friend to meditate each day on the divinely inspired words of scripture. Since the earliest centuries of Christianity, church fathers like Ireneaus, Jerome, and Augustine, took full advantage of this truth. Jerome, a fourth century father who is most famous for translating the scriptures into the Latin *Vulgate*, stated, "When we pray, it is we who speak with God, but when we read (the Bible) it is God who speaks with us. The soul is fed each day with *lectio divina*."[27] This is why reading, memorizing, savoring, and praying the scriptures are so important to our spiritual journey. Personal exposure to the Bible enables us to commune with God, the Author of the scriptures.

Though reading the Bible is important, meditating on the scriptures we have read is even more beneficial. This being the case, understanding meditation in the context of reading scripture should be a top priority. The psalmist declares that we should meditate on the scriptures "day and night," and that doing so will make us "like trees planted by streams of water that yield fruit in season" (Psalm 1:2-3). Perhaps you have reaped the benefits of meditating on scripture, or the concept may seem completely foreign at the moment.

Unfortunately, the word "meditation" has taken on a negative connotation for years, but when one understands the value of meditating on

---

[26] Gregory the Great. *Epist*. IV, 31.

[27] Quoted in Mariano Magrassi. *Praying the Bible: An Introduction to Lectio Divina*. (Collegeville, MN: Liturgical Press, 1998), 15.

the words of God, one's prayer life often becomes richer. Meditating on scripture enables us to claim the promises of God and verbalize them back to him. Meditating on scripture can enable us to witness how God forgave sinners, met needs, performed miracles, and overcame sin, death, and hell. It also reminds us that nothing can separate us from God's presence and love.

I am convinced that we need to hear from God by reading the Bible before allowing God to hear from us through prayer. If you will spend time reading and meditating on scripture, I believe you will discover that your prayer life will become richer in the process. Because reading God's words can encourage, convict, challenge, and transform our thinking, it makes sense to read scripture before praying. It also makes sense to pray while you are reading scripture. Because our thoughts are often scattered, even when trying to pray, meditating on scripture can place our attention on God's words instead of our wandering thoughts.

It is certainly wise to say a prayer just before reading scripture, but communion with God is often richer when one allows God to start the conversation. John Cassian, a contemporary of Augustine in the fourth century, commented on the importance of reading scripture in preparation to pray:

> The praying spirit is shaped by its earlier condition, so therefore before we pray, we must hasten to drive from our heart's sanctuary anything we would not wish to intrude on our prayers.[28]

This is why reading the Bible prior to praying can transform our thought process in preparation to pray. Since we often don't know what to pray, why not read scripture before praying? Reading and meditating on scripture will inevitably lead to prayer because God

---

[28] John Cassian. *Conferences.* trans. Colm Luibheid. (New York: Paulist Press, 1985), 102-103

speaks to us through the divinely inspired words of the Bible. Reading scripture also reminds us of God's mighty power, sovereignty, grace, love, holiness, and unchanging nature, which can only lead to a response of prayer and praise.

Believers of every generation have realized the value of meditating on scripture. Below are some suggestions to encourage your meditation on scripture.

Suggestions for How to Meditate on Scripture

1. Select a passage of scripture.

2. Plan to use a journal or paper to write out your thoughts and questions as you read, reflect, and pray. You may also plan to write out your prayers.

3. Ask God to impact your mind and heart through your reading.

4. Try meditating quietly or choosing to read and pray aloud in order to focus better on communion with God. Either way, try reading the verse or passage slowly and repeatedly.

5. As you read, think about context. Who is the author? Who is being addressed? What is the setting and what is the theme of the story? You may want to utilize a study Bible, Bible dictionary, or Bible commentary for insight about context. Imagine what the author and persons in the story were thinking or feeling.

6. Think about how you might apply God's truth revealed in the passage to your daily life and witness.

Though the Psalms and Gospels are often most conducive to meditation, you can focus on other parts of the scriptures as well. In order to provide you a sense of what this might look like, I have provided a couple passages I've meditated on in the past, as well as the reflections I wrote in my prayer journal.

You keep in perfect peace whose mind is stayed on you, because he trusts in you (Isaiah 26:3, ESV).

My reflections: God, forgive me for worrying about things I cannot control. Thank you for always being in control of all things. Thank you for reminding me through this passage written by the prophet Isaiah centuries ago that if I focus on you, you will give me peace. Help me to trust you today, Lord.

For I am convinced that neither death nor life, neither angels nor demons, neither the present nor the future, nor any powers, neither height nor depth, nor anything else in all creation, will be able to separate us from the love of God that is in Christ Jesus our Lord (Romans 8:38-39).

My reflections: Heavenly Father, I am grateful for your never ending love and provision. Forgive me for being distracted by temptation and the temporary things of this world. No matter what challenges I may face today, Lord, I know that nothing can separate me from your love and grace. Please help me model your love and grace for everyone you bring into my path today.

CHAPTER 18
The Lord's Prayer

Prayer was a way of life for Jesus. The occasions for his prayers were many and varied. He prayed in the early morning and also late at night (Matt. 1:35; 14:23). He frequently prayed alone, and sometimes with others (John 6:15). He prayed during one of his miracles (John 11:41-42). He prayed while blessing meals (Luke 9:16, 24:30; Matt. 15:36; 26:26-27) and also to bless and heal people (Matt. 19:13-15; Luke 27:50). Before selecting his twelve disciples, Jesus "went out to a mountainside to pray, and spent the night praying to God" (Luke 6:12). Since it was necessary for Jesus regularly to spend time during the day and night praying, we must "let Christ's example be a spur inciting us to amend our leisurely approach to prayer." [29]

Prayer preceded major decisions in Jesus's life, as evidenced throughout the New Testament. His decision to leave Capernaum and preach "in the other cities" also followed prayer in "a lonely place" (Mark 1:35; Luke 4:42-43). He prayed in the Garden of Gethsemane the night before his crucifixion (Luke 22:41-42). While hanging on the cross Jesus offered a prayer of forgiveness for his persecutors (Luke 23:34).

---

[29] John Calvin. *Sermons on the Beatitudes: Five Sermons from the Gospel Harmony, Delivered in Geneva in 1560.* trans. by Robert White (Edinburgh: Banner of Truth Trust, 2006), 8-9.

Not only did Jesus lead by example, he also instructed his disciples specifically how to pray. On an occasion after his disciples observed him praying, one said, "Lord, teach us to pray." The response of Jesus has come to be known as "the Lord's Prayer" (Matthew 6:9-13; Luke 11:1-4 KJV):

> Our Father, who art in heaven, hallowed be thy Name. Thy kingdom come, thy will be done, on earth as it is in heaven. Give us this day our daily bread, and forgive us our trespasses, as we forgive those who trespass against us. And lead us not into temptation but deliver us from evil. For thine is the kingdom, and the power, and the glory, for ever and ever. Amen.[30]

By understanding and praying the Lord's Prayer we are allowing the very words of King Jesus to guide our prayers. Because every Christian is a disciple of Christ, his response to his earliest followers applies to us as well. Many people throughout history understood this to be true and enjoyed the benefits of praying the Lord's Prayer. Commenting on the significance of the Lord's Prayer throughout his life, Martin Luther declared, "It is the very best prayer, even better than the psalter, which is so very dear to me." Luther also said, "Every time you are tempted you should go running to the Lord's Prayer."[31] The Lord's Prayer is recited by millions during chapel services and daily Mass worldwide. It is a prescribed part of the Daily Office within the *Book of Common Prayer* as well.

The Lord's Prayer can be divided into two halves: the first part focuses on God, our Father who art in heaven—hallowed be thy name,

---

[30] *The Book of Common Prayer*. (New York: Church Publishing Incorporated, 1979), 54.

[31] Luther's Works: *Devotional Writings II*, edited by Gustav Wiencke. (Philadelphia: Fortress Press, 1968), 200.

may thy will be done on earth as it is in heaven. Then it shifts more to us—give us our daily bread, forgive us our trespasses, lead us not into temptation, but deliver us from evil. The prayer ends essentially where it started, focusing solely on God—for thine is the kingdom, the power, and the glory forever. Martyn Lloyd-Jones correctly points out that the Lord's Prayer is comprehensive and shows us in outline form all that we ought to pray for, with the priority being God's will first, and our needs second. Lloyd-Jones states, "It is a perfect synopsis of our Lord's instruction on how to pray, and what to pray for."[32]

Because Jesus was perfect and never sinned, rather than praying this prayer himself, he gave it to his followers as the best example of how they should pray. For centuries, Christians have offered this prayer to God, saying Christ's words back to him, which make it unique and powerful. The second century document called the *Didache* instructed believers to pray the Lord's Prayer three times per day, and also before Communion and baptisms. When we say this prayer to God, like all other prayers, God already knows what we need before we express it, yet he gave this prayer as a guide for praying.

Questions for Reflection

What are your thoughts about the Lord's Prayer? Is this prayer part of your personal time of prayer or recited during corporate services you participate in?

Are there other prescribed prayers you pray? What might the value be of memorizing these prayers and praying them on a daily basis?

---

[32] Martin Lloyd-Jones. *Studies in the Sermon on the Mount, Vol. 2.* (Grand Rapids: Eerdmans, 1999 reprint), 48.

CHAPTER 19
Praying the Psalms

Sometimes it seems easier or better not to follow instructions. Building Legos sets were a big deal around our house over the years. Our boys couldn't wait to open the sets and get started. We had seen movies and commercials, and even read books about Legos. Each time we started the construction process, our enthusiasm and overconfidence caused us to ignore, and sometimes lose, the instructions. It was as if we believed doing things our way was somehow better than the intentions of the designer of the Legos sets. Eventually, frustration and disappointment were the end result every time. It wasn't for a lack of trying. The answer to our problem was always to go back to the instructions. Our lives are very similar.

There is nothing more important than lives being built to worship and honor God. True knowledge of God arises from a real relationship, just as knowledge of a person does. True knowledge of oneself comes only through a relationship with God. After all, the Triune God created us, and has provided instructions about who we are and how we are supposed to receive instructions in order to flourish in life. We can try to make it work on our own, but the end result will be disappointment and failure. We need to follow the instructions of the great Designer. The Book of Psalms can be viewed as God's instructions to teach us how to pray.

Prayerful

The Book of Psalms, or "Psalter," is considered to be the Prayer Book of the Bible. The psalms, which were originally sung, have helped generation after generation to pray. The psalms are not arranged by topic but flow the way life often does, out of order. One day we praise, the next we complain. Sometimes we cry out, while at other times feel numb. The full range of human emotion is contained in the Book of Psalms—sorrow, joy, pain, lament, thanksgiving, worry, anger, frustration, fear, doubt, hope, peace, and praise. The psalms reveal the character of God and his creatures. They also reveal how God relates to his creatures and how we are to relate to him.

In the psalms we see the recounting of the steadfast love of God (hesed) over and over. The Book of Psalms is the longest book in the Bible. It is broken into five books or divisions that correlate to the five books of the Torah (Genesis, Exodus, Leviticus, Numbers, and Deuteronomy). These five divisions of the Book of Psalms all end with a blessing and praise to God. The first two psalms set the scene, with Psalm 1 centering on knowing God by meditating on the scriptures. The last five psalms (146-150) are all praises. As we center on God's words in the psalms, we will be reminded of his greatness, love, grace, and forgiveness as well. The divisions proceed like so:

- Book One - Psalms 1-41
- Book Two - Psalms 42-72
- Book Three - Psalms 73-89
- Book Four - Psalms 90-1106
- Book Five - Psalms 107-150

Reading the psalms consistently allows us to learn the language used by the biblical writers as a way to form our own prayers to God. Reading the psalms daily helps us navigate life, just as it did for the Israelites as they went on their way. Just as we learned language by listening and imitating, the psalms give us language to listen to and imitate as we learn to pray. The end goal, of course, is to know and worship God. Praise may not come easily or quickly, but eventually prayers pursued far enough will become praise.[33]

Generation after generation have benefited from the psalms. The New Testament has explicit references to the psalms, including the instance when Jesus quoted a psalm while dying on the cross (Psalm 22:1). The apostle Paul encouraged the believers at Ephesus to sing the psalms (Ephesians 5:18-19). The psalms were quoted frequently by the Church Fathers and have played an important role in the lives of great leaders over the centuries. St. Augustine knew the psalms by heart, as reflected throughout *The Confessions*. During the last ten days of his life, Augustine wanted to be left entirely alone. His only request was to have the psalms of David copied out and hung on the walls of his room. Augustine's desire was to spend his final days gazing at and praying the psalms.[34]

Dietrich Bonhoeffer read the psalms every day for years, and once said, "I know them and love them more than any other book."[35] Charles Spurgeon, Billy Graham, and many other influential Christian leaders read the psalms daily as well. It is common for Benedictine monks to sing all 150 psalms every week! Given that there are one hundred and fifty psalms, choosing to read, pray, or sing five psalms per day would enable a person to make it through the entire book of psalms in a month and twelve times in a year. In addition to the Bible, the majority of hymnals and prayer books contain portions of psalms and can therefore be utilized to aid a person's time of prayer as well. Praying the psalms helps us to understand them, as well as the One to whom we belong.

---

[33] Eugene H. Peterson. *Answering God: The Psalms as Tools for Prayer*. (New York: HarperCollins, 1989), 127.

[34] Augustine. *The Confessions*. Quoted in the preface by Patricia Hampl. (New York: Vintage, 1998), xxvi.

[35] Dietrich Bonhoeffer. *Letters & Papers from Prison*. ed. by Eberhard Bethge. (New York: Touchstone, 1971), 40.

Prayerful

Actions for Reflection

Perhaps you have a favorite psalm. Choose one and rewrite it in your own words.

Practice writing a psalm of thanksgiving, lament, confession, or praise.

CHAPTER 20
Prayers of Lament

During childhood we discover that life isn't fair. At some point in life, people who believe in God, or are agnostic, ask one of two questions of God when facing difficult circumstances: 1) "Lord, where are you?" 2) "God, are you and your plan for me really good?" These questions found their origin in the Garden of Eden when the devil posed them to the first humans. The enemy doubted God's goodness, words, plan, and relationship with Adam and Eve (Genesis 3). So goes the story, the man and woman created in God's image decided to abandon God's truth in favor of the enemy's lies. They disobeyed God, and the devastating consequences of their sinful actions are still being felt today. The realization of the damage caused by their sin has often resulted in prayers of "lament."

The word lament means "to wail, protest, cry out or complain." It's not pretty. Think of a mother in labor, lamenting the pain of childbearing, or the newborn baby crying out in the coldness as she emerges from the warmth of her mother's womb. Those images of lament help us to learn what prayerful worship should be about. The pain and disappointment we experience in this world can actually serve as a lamenting prayer offered to express our disappointment with this world and our longing for home.

Lament is actually a gift meant to hold our hearts until we reach heaven. There would be no benefit for a woman to remain silent when giving birth, or a newborn not to cry when first exposed to the bright lights and noise of the world. Likewise, rather than assuming we should remain silent, not complain, and just grin and bear the pain experienced in this world, we should cry out to God during our times of desperation.

God does not want us to live in fear, but in love. If we love someone, we know it's okay to complain to them. When we know they love us unconditionally, it brings joy knowing that they actually desire to share in our highs and lows. It's the reason why traditional marriage vows include the promise to love in sickness and in health, whether rich or poor, during good times and bad. Regardless of circumstances, God loves us and wants us to share every aspect of our lives with him.

The prayers of lament mentioned in the Bible teach us that it is not only alright to complain to God, but necessary. We also learn that we can ask for what we need with confidence as we remember God loves and cares for us. Prayers of lament enable us to cry out to God, express our frustrations, confess our sins, realize his greatness, and trust in his provision.

Dozens of psalms exhibit prayers of lament. The entire Book of Lamentations, along with portions of other biblical writings (Job, Jeremiah, and Ezekiel), contain prayers of lament. The night before his crucifixion, Jesus offered a prayer of lament (Matthew 26:36-46). He also expressed lament while hanging on a cross the following day (Psalm 22).

There are four basic elements present within a prayer of lament: 1) Calling out to God, 2) Issuing a complaint, 3) Making a request, and 4) Trusting God. A prayer of lament begins by coming to the end of our own reasoning and calling out to God. Then, we offer up our complaint about what is happening and how it goes against what we know to be true about and of God. Third, we ask God for what we want and need. We should conclude the prayer of lament with confession, praise, and trust, knowing that we need God's grace, can give thanks for past provision, and trust in what he will provide in the future.

In addition to the entire Book of Job, another great example of lament is found in Psalm 77, which was written by a man named Asaph experiencing his darkest of days:

> 1 I cried out to God for help;
> I cried out to God to hear me.
> 2 When I was in distress, I sought the Lord;
> at night I stretched out untiring hands,
> and I would not be comforted.
> 3 I remembered you, God, and I groaned;
> I meditated, and my spirit grew faint.
> 4 You kept my eyes from closing;
> I was too troubled to speak.
> 5 I thought about the former days,
> the years of long ago;
> 6 I remembered my songs in the night.
> My heart meditated, and my spirit asked:
> 7 "Will the Lord reject forever?
> Will he never show his favor again?
> 8 Has his unfailing love vanished forever?
> Has his promise failed for all time?
> 9 Has God forgotten to be merciful?
> Has he in anger withheld his compassion?"
> 10 Then I thought, "To this I will appeal:
> the years when the Most High stretched out his right hand.
> 11 I will remember the deeds of the Lord;
> yes, I will remember your miracles of long ago.
> 12 I will consider all your works
> and meditate on all your mighty deeds."

13 Your ways, God, are holy.
    What god is as great as our God?
14 You are the God who performs miracles;
    you display your power among the peoples.
15 With your mighty arm you redeemed your people,
    the descendants of Jacob and Joseph.
16 The waters saw you, God,
    the waters saw you and writhed;
    the very depths were convulsed.
17 The clouds poured down water,
    the heavens resounded with thunder;
    your arrows flashed back and forth.
18 Your thunder was heard in the whirlwind,
    your lightning lit up the world;
    the earth trembled and quaked.
19 Your path led through the sea,
    your way through the mighty waters,
    though your footprints were not seen.
20 You led your people like a flock
    by the hand of Moses and Aaron.

In verses 1-4, Asaph calls out to God at a time when he was too troubled to speak or move. There will be times in life when we feel beyond weary, even to the point of being paralyzed. In verses 5-9, Asaph issues a complaint, questioning God's compassion, nature, and care for him at a time when needed most. His lament gives us permission to ask questions of the Lord as well. God can take whatever we want to gripe about, for he already knows how we feel. Verses 10-20 show a shift in Asaph's thinking and words, going from despair to hope, remembering God's promises, offering praise, and trusting in God's faithfulness to provide once more.

As we offer prayers of lament during the darkest of days, in the midst of grief and despair, God will offer a ray of hope to lead us back into his loving arms and gracious provision. The Lord does not expect us to be silent during our pain. Lament allows us to cry out in sorrow, express our pain, remember God's promises, and trust in his goodness to serve as the anchor of our souls during the turbulent storms and navigation through troubled waters. After all, Jesus said from the cross during his darkest hour, "My God, my God, why have you forsaken me," which was a quote from Psalm 22. Jesus also calmed a storm and walked on water. He has been through and conquered everything we may face in life or death. He promises to lead us beside still waters, prepare a table before us even in the presence of our enemies, walk with us through the valley of the shadow of death, and allow us to dwell with him forever (Psalm 23).

Actions for Reflection

Practice writing your own prayer of lament. There are no wrong words or ways. The formula is simple, and the invitation is given to everyone.

1. Call out to God.
2. Protest your pain, confusion, fear, or whatever else you need to complain about.
3. Make your request to God.
4. Remember and proclaim who you know God to be. Trust in God's provision.

CHAPTER 21
Free and Formed Prayers

If you were to say the exact same thing to a close friend or family member every time you speak with them, the communication and relationship might seem shallow, superficial, or disingenuous. No one communicates this way, unless of course they are working a job that has trained them to respond in the same way, perhaps with a phrase like, "It's my pleasure." The person may be sincere, but it can seem a little forced. I've found humor in trying to mix it up with questions or comments that might cause those employees to ditch the canned phrases. Might it be a good idea for us to let our prayers flow beyond the same phrases from time to time as well? It is not that we should not pray the same prayers. Rather, we should also consider praying exactly what's on our mind and heart, just as we would when communicating with our closest friends. After all, God already knows what we are thinking anyway.

Should we value prescribed prayers over spontaneous prayers? If the prescribed prayers contain the inspired words of God recorded in the scriptures, of course we should revere them more than anything we can come up with. I've found that when I am distracted, praying the scriptures helps me focus on the Lord and eternal things, which in turn leads to more fruitful praying. Praying the scriptures can help us rehearse prayer, while also providing us with God's words to pray when we cannot come up with our own. Finding balance is important. At the end of the day, we should acknowledge that God has given us the scriptures to guide our prayers, while also realizing that we can communicate exactly what is on our heart and mind. I have found that the fruit of spontaneous prayer will often result from praying in the garden of prescribed prayers.

When you spend enough time hearing a person pray, you will realize that everyone prays both free and formed prayers. The *Book of Common Prayer* prescribes many beautiful, powerful prayers for believers to pray, and most of them are tied directly to scripture.[36] I will list some in a moment. Though some may object to the idea of praying a prescribed prayer, studying the Bible and history of Christianity should eliminate any concerns. After all, the Lord's Prayer is a prescribed prayer! It is also important to remember that even though Jesus himself prayed the scriptures, he also prayed spontaneous prayers. This being the case, it seems that we should utilize the scriptures and also rely on the Holy Spirit to guide our spontaneous prayers.

Millions of Christians have experienced the richness of praying formed prayers for centuries. Though Catholics, Anglicans, Episcopalians, and those in the Greek Orthodox tradition frequently utilize formed prayers, Christians of all traditions say similar prayers before congregations, meals, and bedtime on a regular basis. What matters more than the choice between praying free or formed prayers is the substance of the prayers (being biblically based) and the intentions of the one praying. Below is an example of a prescribed prayer (a prayer of thanksgiving) found in the *Book of Common Prayer* that could be useful during your daily time of prayer:

---

[36] In addition to prescribing prayers for many special occasions and times throughout the liturgical year, the *Book of Common Prayer* contains prayers translated from the Latin by 16th century theologian Thomas Cramner that many Christians utilize each week.

Almighty God, Father of all mercies,
we your unworthy servants give you humble thanks
for all your goodness and loving-kindness
to us and to all whom you have made.
We bless you for our creation, preservation,
and all the blessings of this life;
but above all for your immeasurable love
in the redemption of the world by our Lord Jesus Christ;
for the means of grace, and for the hope of glory.
And, we pray, give us such an awareness of your mercies,
that with truly thankful hearts we may show forth your praise,
not only with our lips, but in our lives,
by giving up ourselves to your service,
and by walking before you
in holiness and righteousness all our days;
through Jesus Christ our Lord,
to whom, with you and the Holy Spirit,
be honor and glory throughout all ages. Amen.[37]

There are many prayers recorded in the New Testament that could also be utilized during your daily time of prayer (Ephesians 3:14-20; Hebrews 13:20-21; 1 Peter 1:3-5 and Jude 24-25).

In addition to utilizing the Lord's Prayer as a model to guide our prayers, many influential Christians over the centuries have also used the Ten Commandments and Apostles' Creed to serve as guides for daily prayer as well. One way in which the early Christians defended the faith against heresy was by developing creeds, each serving as a symbol, or defense, of orthodoxy. The Apostles' Creed listed below,

---

[37] *The Book of Common Prayer.* (New York: Church Publishing Incorporated, 1979). This prayer is recited every day by thousands of Christians around the world.

which has undergone slight changes since the first version appeared in the second century, provides an excellent summary of basic Christian doctrine. It has served as the standard ecumenical creed for centuries, and to this day is repeated in chapel and church services by millions of people worldwide on a weekly basis. It can serve as a guide to your prayers as well.

The Apostles' Creed

> I believe in God, the Father almighty,
> Creator of heaven and earth.
> I believe in Jesus Christ, his only Son, our Lord,
> who was conceived by the Holy Spirit,
> born of the Virgin Mary,
> suffered under Pontius Pilate,
> was crucified, died and was buried;
> he descended into hell;
> on the third day he rose again from the dead;
> he ascended into heaven,
> and is seated at the right hand of God the Father almighty;
> from there he will come to judge the living and the dead.
> I believe in the Holy Spirit,
> the holy catholic church,
> the communion of saints,
> the forgiveness of sins,
> the resurrection of the body,
> and the life everlasting.
> Amen.

Questions for Reflection

What are your thoughts about the Apostles' Creed? Why might it be useful to memorize and recite within your daily prayers?

Are there prescribed prayers that you pray on a regular basis? Do you believe one should value prescribed prayers over spontaneous prayers, or vice versa?

CHAPTER 22
Praying for Others

It wasn't until graduate school that I realized the importance of praying consistently for others. About once per month my wife and I would take our elderly relatives to dinner. Ted and Helen were in their early nineties, had trouble hearing, and lived in an apartment full of religious artwork that had been accumulated during seventy years of marriage. Our conversations always revolved around their love for God, the Bible, and people coming to Christ. On each occasion, Ted and Helen would share their desire to die and be with Jesus. Being in my early twenties, hearing them talk about longing for death seemed a little weird. Over time I came to realize that they were serious about longing to see Jesus face to face. Following dinner one evening, I decided to ask Ted and Helen why they thought God would allow them to keep living even though they were so ready to die and be with him.

I'll never forget their response. Ted picked up the large print Bible from the coffee table, opened it, and then pulled out a piece of paper and asked my wife and I to look over the names written on the page. To our surprise, about midway down the sheet were our names. Ted then said, "Helen and I pray for you and every person on this prayer list every day, sometimes multiple times per day. Don't you think that is enough of a reason for the Lord to allow us to keep living in our old age?" It was also a blessing to hear Ted say, "Prayer is a privilege and powerful gift that God has given us to utilize and enjoy. Our job is to be faithful in prayer for you and the others on this list each day. For we know that God is always working through our prayers."

It is interesting how much we can learn about praying by being around prayerful people. When I was a young parent with small children, Saturday mornings were the only day of the week in which I might get a little extra sleep. One particular weekend I remember my son nudging me to wake up on a day when I hoped to sleep longer. Knowing it was time to get up, I asked Jake if he would go downstairs to find out what mommy was making for breakfast. After being gone a few minutes, he returned without an answer. I then urged him to go back downstairs to ask again. When he returned the second time and could not provide an answer, I asked him, "What did mommy say about breakfast?" Jake replied, "I did not ask her!" Being a little frustrated and hungry, I said, "Why not?" His response was, "I did not want to interrupt mommy because she was praying." At only four years old, my son knew the importance of his mother spending time with God each morning. He also knew that his mother was praying for him.

God works through prayer, especially persistent prayers. St. Augustine's mother, Monica, was a devout Christian who prayed fervently for her son's conversion for many years, sometimes through tears. Though Augustine lived in constant rebellion, she never stopped praying for his salvation. In 383 AD, when Augustine wanted to go to Rome to pursue a legal career, his mother clung to him and refused to let him go out of fear that he would drift further into sin. Sadly, Augustine told his mother that she could accompany him to Rome, but then lied and ended up sailing away without her. Little did Monica know, but in Italy God would answer her prayers for Augustine's salvation. He would go on to be one of the most influential Christians in history. It is a prime example of the importance of being faithful to pray for those God has placed in our lives.

Just as each family needs prayer as the foundation upon which to flourish, so do churches. Congregations filled with prayerless people, especially leaders neglecting prayer, will eventually not have many people. Clergy neglecting the office of prayer are like a shepherd abandoning their sheep. Nineteenth-century minister Charles Spurgeon had a congregation of ten thousand people. He knew every member by name and personally baptized each one. He also preached multiple times per week, started orphanages, trained ministers, and to this day is one of the most widely published authors in the English language. When asked how he was able to be a faithful husband and father, as well as one of the most influential leaders England had ever known, Spurgeon replied, "My people pray for me."

Questions for Reflection

Is anyone praying for you on a regular basis? If so, how often do you communicate with them? If not, who might you ask to pray for you daily?

If you were to keep a prayer list, what names and needs would you include? If you are a parent, do you pray for your children daily? If you are a teacher, do you pray for your students?

Do the people closest to you know that you pray for them? If not, how might this become a priority for you?

CHAPTER 23
Praying for Enemies

It's much easier to pray for friends and family than those we are tempted to despise. God knew this would be the case, which is why Jesus gave specific advice about praying for our enemies: "You have heard it said, 'Love your neighbor and hate your enemy.' But I tell you: Love your enemies and pray for those who persecute you" (Matthew 5:43-45). After reflecting on this command, the eleventh-century Archbishop of Canterbury, Anselm, responded with the following prayer for his enemies:

> You (God), who are true light, lighten their darkness;
> You, who are whole truth, correct their errors;
> You, who are true life, give life to their souls. [38]

Nine centuries later, when Europe was on the brink of WWII, Oxford professor C.S. Lewis explained to a friend how he learned to pray for Hitler and Stalin, two world leaders responsible for millions of deaths in the years that would follow:

---

[38] Quoted in B. Jeffrey Bingham. *Pocket History of the Church*. (Downers Grove, IL: InterVarsity Press, 2002), 81.

> When you pray for Hitler and Stalin how do you actually teach yourself to make the prayer real? The two things that help me are: "A continual grasp of the idea that one is only joining one's feeble little voice to the perpetual intercession of Christ who died for these very men" and.... "You and I are not at bottom so different from these ghastly creatures."[39]

When we realize that it is only God's grace that provides true forgiveness for every person willing to embrace it, our desire to pray for "enemies" should increase. Rather than wishing for the demise of their enemies, Anselm and Lewis prayed for their salvation. In order to follow the command of Jesus to love our enemies, we should strive to pray for our enemies as well. Because at times this may seem impossible, we must ask God for help.

There is no better example than Christ's example. While nailed to a cross, being tortured by his enemies, Jesus prayed, "Father, forgive them, for they do not know what they are doing" (Luke 23:34). Several decades later, St. James, who led the early church in Jerusalem and penned a New Testament letter bearing his name, uttered the same words of forgiveness as he was being executed for his faith.

Perhaps you have heard the phrase, "Keep your friends close and your enemies closer?" This phrase has been interpreted in a variety of ways. One thing I have discovered to be true is that it is much harder to be angry with people I am praying for. Because scripture commands us to love and pray for everyone, consider writing down the names of the "enemies" in your life, and ask God to help you extend the mercy and grace that have been shown to you. Forgiveness is a choice, and those choosing not to forgive are choosing to stay angry. It's why the apostle Paul said, "don't let the sun go down on your anger" (Ephesians 4:26).

---

[39] *Letters of C.S. Lewis* (16 April 1940), Edited by W.H. Lewis. (New York: Harcourt, 1966), 183.

When people choose to forgive, they are choosing to live in peace, instead of the bondage that accompanies holding grudges.

Imagine how different churches, neighborhoods, cities, and nations might be if we sincerely committed ourselves to praying for leaders, ministers, politicians, sports rivals, and a variety of others who we dislike or tend to criticize. To take it a step further, we should commit to praying for everyone we want to criticize. It's one thing to pray for friends and family, and another to pray for those we dislike. God can change anyone. Why not pray for our enemies to become our friends? Praying the Lord's Prayer can help, especially when we ask the Lord to "forgive us our trespasses as we forgive those who trespass against us." May God help us to forgive and pray for our "enemies."

Questions for Reflection

As difficult as it may seem to do, can you think of "enemies" you can pray for in the coming days?

Think about the Lord's Prayer stating that we should forgive others as we have been forgiven. Because God died for us while we were "enemies" living in our sins (Romans 5:10), can you think of a specific way to show forgiveness to someone who has wronged you?

CHAPTER 24
Keeping a Prayer Journal

One of my closest friends has a simple way to chart prayer requests (and answers) that anyone can emulate. Using a spiral notebook, he writes the names of each friend and family member at the top of a page. One page is designated for each person. As prayer requests are shared, he writes them down, along with the dates in which the need was first conveyed. As he communicates weekly with the beneficiaries of his daily prayers, he then writes updates in the margin next to every prayer request. When God answers a prayer, he records the date when the prayer request was fulfilled. This method has numerous benefits, including the joy of experiencing God working through prayer, as well as the timing and ways in which specific requests were answered.

I had never really thought much about writing down prayer requests until attending seminary. During one of my first courses, which was a five-day winter term, my professor began each class period inviting students to share prayer requests. Since I had spent my undergraduate years at a secular institution, sharing prayer requests publicly or keeping a prayer list seemed a little weird—even though I was now attending a seminary. Besides, this was a theology class, and I was ready to learn about theology and doctrine, not how to have some type of counseling session where people could share their problems. During the first day of class I was a little surprised to hear a dozen students mention prayer requests, and even more so when the professor took time to write down each petition. This guy was serious about prayer! After ten minutes and several glances at my watch, I wondered if we would ever get on with learning about the Bible.

After the professor asked for the thirteenth time if anyone else had a prayer request to share, a long pause ensued before a student on the front row partially stood up and faced the class. His large hearing aids and slurred speech made me realize that he was hearing impaired. He apologized for his reluctance to share his need. He also apologized for his speech impediment, and then mentioned that normally he didn't have so much trouble hearing, but that his hearing aids were old and no longer working very well. Literally in tears, he mentioned that he felt so helpless and discouraged about becoming the preacher God called him to be because he could not hear and therefore could not learn what was necessary during his time of training. The professor asked him the cost of new hearing aids, to which my fellow student said it would be about $4000. I was broke, like most other seminary students, but really wanted to provide monetary support for my classmate. The professor then placed his hand on the student and asked us to join him in prayer.

At that moment I really felt convicted about having been so lax about prayer and initially bothered by the teacher devoting so much of class time to taking prayer requests. From that day forward I made the commitment to write down prayer requests so that I would remember to pray for specific people and needs. The very next day our professor began class by asking the hearing-impaired student to stand beside him. The professor put his hand on the student's shoulder and said to the class:

> Yesterday our brother in Christ was willing to share his need because something was keeping him from learning and

doing his best for God. God knew before the foundation of the world what each of our needs would be today. We have prayed for our brother, and God has done what he planned to do all along (Matthew 6:8).

How blessed we are to have been given the gift of prayer, and to have approached the throne of grace with confidence together. I received a call yesterday from a friend who was in town on business. Over dinner I mentioned to him the specific prayer request that was shared in class yesterday. I am overjoyed to share with you the fact that last night I was given a check for $4000 so that our brother can get the hearing aids he needs in order to be the preacher God has called him to be.

It has been said that a dull pencil remembers more than a sharp mind. No matter how great your memory, you will sometimes forget prayer requests. It is the reason why my professor wrote the requests on the white board.

I have found that keeping a prayer list, perhaps in a journal or as a file on a computer or phone, can help us to remember who and what to pray for each day. It can also serve as a way to look back and chart answered prayers. In addition to writing down prayer requests in a journal, you can also write out specific prayers, perhaps ones prompted by reading and meditating on scripture. I had been a Christian for many years before realizing the importance of making prayer journaling a priority in my daily life. I hope that you will learn to take advantage of this opportunity as well.

Prayerful

Actions for Reflection

Consider using a journal as a way to record your walk with God. Here are some suggestions to guide your writing:

1. After praying and reading scripture, use one paragraph to write out what you learned and what you'd like to say to God, perhaps by writing out a prayer. Then, after spending time reflecting on scripture and listening to what God may be saying to you, use a second paragraph or page to record the thoughts that come to mind.

2. Make a list of people and needs to pray for, and then plan to do a daily, weekly, or monthly review to record how and when God responded to your specific prayers. Be sure to use a dated page for each day you use your journal. You may also devote a page for each person you plan to pray for on a regular basis.

CHAPTER 25
The Importance of Silence, Solitude, and a Place to Pray

Numerous studies have shown that the average person speaks more than 7,000 words per day.[40] When we take into account the words we type and text as well, the opportunities to influence others, both positively and negatively, become even greater. The scriptures declare that there is life and death in the power of our words (Proverbs 18:21). Therefore, we should choose our words wisely. Even a fool can appear wise if silent! As a teacher, talking plays a big role in my daily life. Because teachers exert much influence over the students entrusted to their care, the Bible warns them to be careful with their words (James 3:1). For every believer, words are the chief means by which we communicate with God and others.

Though words are a necessary part of life, they can cause problems, even for those with the best intentions. Many years ago, while standing in a checkout line I asked a lady who seemed pregnant when her baby was due. It was obvious to me that her delivery date was fast approaching. To my shock and great regret, her response was, "I am

---

[40] "Do Women Really Talk More Than Men?" *Psychology Today*, October 10, 2019, https://www.psychologytoday.com/us/blog/marriage-equals/201910/do-women-really-talk-more-men. Accessed Jan 2, 2024. This article claims that most women speak nearly 20,000 words per day.

Prayerful

not pregnant!" It didn't matter that I was simply trying to make polite conversation. Though I apologized profusely, irrevocable damage had been done. My wife told me to go to the car. None of us will forget that dreadful encounter caused by my words. Like toothpaste having been squeezed from a tube, I could not take back my words. I have often regretted my speech, but rarely my silence. There are times in life when silence is necessary and much more beneficial than talking.

Silence can be difficult for those expected to talk. Leaders, by nature of their positions, are always speaking in one way or another. The danger comes when they fail to listen. The same concept can apply to our spiritual lives, for if we develop the habit of not listening to others, we are likely not going to listen to God either. Even when we realize the importance of listening, it can be hard to hear because of the noise that distracts our thoughts, concentration, and ability to hear God. Even venues designed to promote quiet and listening, like movie theaters and libraries, have trouble enforcing policies. Nobody likes it when someone talks loudly in either of those places, unless of course you're the one disturbing the peace. How about the people out in public talking on speakerphone so everyone can hear their conversation? You get the point.

In addition to the noise caused by others, many of us have allowed personal choices to prevent our ability to listen. Few days go by without having music playing, the television on, my phone in hand, or simply being around people during every waking hour. In this current generation, statistics show that the average person devotes at least six hours per day engaged in some form of digital media, whether it be a smartphone, computer screen, or other electronic device.[41] Silence is not only a rarity for many people, but also makes some people uncomfortable to the point of avoiding silence during

---

[41] "Tech Addiction by the Numbers: How Much Time We Spend Online." PC, https://www.pcmag.com/news/tech-addiction-by-the-numbers-how-much-time-we-spend-online. Accessed January 8, 2024. "Average Time Spent Per Day with Digital Media in the US from 2011 to 2024."

the day and even sleeping with some type of background noise throughout the night. In and of themselves, these examples may not be bad. However, we must not deceive ourselves into thinking that noise does not prevent our ability to concentrate, learn, and hear from God. So, whether the noise and distractions are self-imposed, or the result of others and loud environments, how can we cultivate lives conducive to hearing from God? Silence and solitude can help remedy the problem.

It can be hard to hear anyone when we are talking, which means sometimes we need to be quiet. Just as it becomes difficult for two people to hear one another when talking at the same time, why would it be any different with God? Even though we can be silent, the world around us may not be. There will be times when the only way to escape the noise is to get away. Jesus spent forty days in the desert with the heavenly Father before starting his earthly ministry (Matthew 4:1-11). Though he loved and spent much time with crowds, the scriptures contain numerous examples of him spending time alone in prayer (Matthew 14:23; 17:1-9; 26:36-46; Mark 1:35; Luke 5:16; 6:12).

During the earliest centuries of Christianity, which were sometimes marked by persecution, heresy, and spiritual lethargy, monks escaped to the desert to eliminate distractions and seek God. Monasticism blossomed during the fourth century when a monk named Antony sold a fortune in order to pursue God fully in the desert. He spent most days praying and reading only the Bible. Rather than viewing solitude as a way to neglect ministry, Antony believed it was essential preparation to serve others. Other monks followed, and their example of holiness led thousands to the desert, including Emperor Constantine and his sons, seeking advice and prayer.

What Antony was to monasticism in the East, Benedict of Nursia was to Western Monasticism a century and a half later. Like Antony, Benedict gave up wealth to pursue God in a cave. Others followed, including his sister, Scholastica, who founded a similar community for women. Chief among their disciplines was prayer. In addition to reading the scriptures and reciting psalms, praying eight times was the daily norm. They pointed to scripture to justify their actions (Psalm 119:62; 119:164). In subsequent centuries, many other saints drew closer to God and were better prepared to serve others through utilizing "Benedict's Rules," which included the disciplines of silence and solitude.

Legendary nun Mother Teresa of Calcutta knew the importance of silence and solitude during prayer. When famous television personality Dan Rather once asked her about what she says to God, Teresa replied, "I listen." As you think about your daily life in general, and times of prayer in particular, how often do you take time to listen? I know it can be hard amid all the noise, but it is possible. A friend of mine, who happens to be a rabbi, once shared the significant role silence plays within his household during every Sabbath. When the sun goes down each Friday, his wife and children turn off all electronic devices, and even place phones and any other potential distractions into a basket. The ensuing hours are spent in silence, singing psalms, and reciting prayers. Rather than feeling deprived, everyone in his household looks forward to this weekly privilege.

If Jesus, his earliest followers, and countless others over the years had to be intentional about seeking silence and solitude, why would it be any less important for us to do the same? At times, everyone needs to be alone. I love my family but realize the importance of spending quality time alone with God each day. When I don't, it is obvious to everyone. This may look a little different for each person. My friend JD leaves his office each day for a brief walk around the block in order to gather his thoughts, pray, and listen to God. My friend Tim starts every morning on his patio with prayer, his Bible, a cigar and cup of coffee.

In addition to having a designated time of silence and solitude each day, setting aside longer periods of time to benefit from these disciplines can only strengthen one's spiritual journey. We must learn not only to tell God what is on our hearts, but also take time to ask God what is on his heart. My friend Paul spends several days each year at a monastery in the mountains of California in order to pray, read the scriptures, and listen to God.

What might an extended period of silence and solitude look like for you? You may not be able to go to the mountains or a desert in order to escape the distractions, but silence and solitude can be found if you seek it. Awakening early or staying up later than others can provide uninterrupted, quiet time with God. I have also learned to take advantage of time spent in the car during the daily commute to work and school in order to commune with God.

God is always speaking, oftentimes much more clearly when we are most intentional about listening. Though God can speak through thunder, an earthquake, mighty wind, or through other circumstances, there will be times when God speaks through a still, small voice, or whisper, like in the case with the prophet Elijah (1 Kings 19:11-3). Based on personal experience and testimonies recorded in the scriptures and history, I am convinced that adopting the spiritual disciplines of silence and solitude will enable you to hear more clearly what God wants to convey to you.

Do you have a designated place to pray? Though one can pray anywhere and anytime, it is often harder to pray amid noise and interruptions. I've had students and teachers from private schools mention that chapel is the only time they pray. It is not coincidental that having a designated time and space provide opportunities most conducive to encountering God. I've known many people who have designated a specific room or closet in their homes for prayer. My friend Mike often utilizes a bathroom in his house as the best place to pray.

Because God is readily available at all times and wants to hear from us, we can pray in a boat, on a subway, standing in Times Square, or countless other places. Regardless of your preference, the key is to pick a spot that enables you to focus best on communicating with

Prayerful

God. Choosing a space free of noise and distractions is usually best. Just as you would devote undivided attention when meeting with someone really important, you should consider turning off your television, phone, computer, or whatever else may distract your daily meetings with the Lord. God desires and deserves your undivided attention, and it will benefit you to provide it.

Questions and Actions for Reflection

As you think about your life, what noises and other voices compete for your attention? Who and what distract you from praying and listening to God?

Consider using silence as a way to fast from words. If you are an extrovert like me, this may be difficult at first, so be sure to set realistic goals. Consider spending at least thirty minutes or an hour not talking. Eventually, spending a whole day or week in silence with God can become possible.

What can you do, and where might you go, in order to cultivate silence and solitude in your daily life? If you don't already have a designated place to pray, find a spot free of distractions and noise in order to spend quality time alone with God. This could be in your car, on the front porch of your house, or somewhere else.

CHAPTER 26
Time to Pray

Many of us feel as though we don't have the time to pray, yet this is exactly why we should pray more than we do. It is not coincidental that all godly persons throughout the ages were people of prayer. Martin Luther devoted at least two hours every day to fervent prayer, as did Jonathan Edwards, John Wesley, Charles Spurgeon, Thomas Merton, Mother Teresa, and countless other leaders God used in mighty ways. What can we learn from their testimonies? That it will be impossible to have a right relationship with God, much less love and serve others as we should, unless we are willing to spend time conversing with God through prayer. It is not a matter of having enough time, for we all have been granted twenty-four hours each day. It has to do with how we manage the time we've been given.

How often should we pray? The apostle Paul urges us to "pray without ceasing" (1 Thessalonians 5:17). Eleventh century Cistercian monk Bernard of Clairvaux wrote, "We must not devote ourselves to prayer once or twice, but frequently, diligently, letting God know the longing of our hearts."[42] Instead of praying only before meals, ball games, or bedtime, we can learn to converse with God throughout the day.

Because the goal is to have an ongoing conversation with God

---

[42] Quoted in B. Jeffrey Bingham, *Pocket History of the Church*. (Downers Grove, IL: InterVarsity Press, 2002), 76.

each day, setting aside specific times to pray will help. This doesn't mean one has to pray eight times per day like Benedictine monks, but it might not be a bad idea, for when we develop a disciplined, consistent pattern, spontaneous prayer will become the natural result. George Whitefield, arguably the greatest evangelist in history, claimed that the power of his preaching resulted from his time in prayer. His diary reveals that he often prayed early in the morning, again at noon, and just before retiring for the day.

Scheduling specific times to pray can help us develop the habit of praying. Of course, we can pray outside of the designated times of prayer in a way similar to speaking or sending a short text to a good friend multiple times throughout the day. Given the busy times in which we live, sometimes a short prayer will be long enough. Though we should say short, simple prayers to God throughout the day, like "help me, forgive me, guard my mouth, give me wisdom, I love you, and thank you," it is also imperative to take time to share and listen more deeply.

People often ask, "When is the best time of the day to pray?" Praying without ceasing was the apostle Paul's response. This may look different from person to person, but based on examples in the scriptures and history, it makes sense for us to pray before our feet hit the ground each morning. The Old Testament prophet Ezekiel mentioned, "In the morning the word of the Lord came to me" (Ezekiel 12:8). King David said, "In the morning, O Lord, you hear my voice; In the morning I lay my requests before you and wait in expectation" (Psalm 5:3). As the Psalmist declared, and theologian Dietrich Bonhoeffer concurred, "the first thought and the first word of the day belong to God."[43] When you awake, let your first words be, "Good morning, Father."

Charles Spurgeon claimed, "It should be our rule never to see the

---

[43] Dietrich Bonhoeffer. *Life Together*. (New York: Harper, 1954), 29.

face of men before first seeing the face of God."⁴⁴ It has been said that the most important meal of the day is breakfast, for it provides us with the energy needed to start the day. Similarly, beginning each day with prayer provides great spiritual benefits. Twentieth-century minister A.W. Tozer also understood the importance of starting each day in communion with God. Reverend Bobby Moore shares a remarkable account:

> When an acquaintance of mine was called to preach in Chicago, A.W. Tozer called him and said, 'This city is a devil's den. It is a very difficult place to minister the Word of God. You will come up against much opposition from the enemy. If you ever want to pray with me, I am at the lakeside every morning at five-thirty. Just make your way down and we can pray together.' Not wanting to bother the great man as he was seeking the Lord, the new minister did not immediately accept his offer. But one day he was so troubled that he made his way very early to the lakeside, about six o'clock, only to find God's servant prostrate upon the sand. Needless to say, he did not disturb him.⁴⁵

We can choose to begin each day communicating with the Lord or attempt to make it on our own. Setting the alarm clock helps me keep my commitment. Even though this is my goal each morning, some days it doesn't happen. Thankfully, God understands, and is ready to listen when I am ready to pray. Without a doubt, I am better prepared for whatever the day may bring when I start it with prayer. Regardless of how tired or busy I can be, I have never regretted time spent with the Lord. I have found it helpful to ask God for guidance and provision in the morning, and then pray for

---

⁴⁴ Bobby Moore. *Your Personal Devotional Life*. (Southaven, MS: The Kings Press, 2004), 4.
⁴⁵ Ibid.

strength, wisdom, and discernment throughout the day. Just before going to bed, I confess any sins God may reveal and then give thanks for all he provided and allowed me to experience during the day.

Think about how you spend the time God has given you. We all make time for the people and things that are important to us. Regardless of how busy or tired we are, we find time to engage in the relationships and activities that we value most. It is all about priorities. Time spent in fervent prayer will never be wasted time because the greatest blessing of prayer is spending time with God. The key is to get started, even if for just a few minutes each day. With intentionality and effort, you will discover that it is possible to build your day around prayer, instead of trying to squeeze prayer into your busy schedule.

Questions for Reflection

If you are not already doing so, when and how can you designate specific times to pray each day?

Are there others in your life who can help you pray more consistently each day? Participating in a daily or a weekly prayer meeting at a local church can help.

CHAPTER 27
Fasting and Other Aids to Prayer

The Bible mentions numerous examples of people fasting in order to draw closer to God. Moses and Elijah fasted for forty days (Exodus 34:28-29; 1 Kings 19:9-12). In both cases, each man abstained from food in order to encounter God and discern instructions about what to do next. The prophet Joel fasted so that he might turn from sin in order to turn to God (Joel 1:14). Jesus fasted for forty days in the wilderness prior to starting his public ministry (Matthew 4:1-11). He expected his followers to fast as well, as noted when he said to them, "*When you fast*, do so not to be seen by men, but by your Father who is in heaven" (Matthew 6:16-18).

Abstaining from food was practiced in order to draw closer to God. In every case, prayer was involved in the time of fasting. The "secret fasting" no doubt drew them closer to God while simultaneously helping them avoid seeking recognition from others. In other words, Jesus wanted them to fast for the right reasons, ultimately to draw closer to God through prayer.

For centuries, Christians have fasted in order to commune with God, especially during Lent, which is a forty-day period that mirrors the time Jesus spent being tempted in the desert (Matthew 4:1-11). Most people choose to give up something they don't want to do without, such as chocolate, cupcakes, wine, or meat. Rather than abstaining from food, I've known some people who have chosen to fast from social media, the news, negative speech, or a host of other things they sensed had become addictive or a hindrance from focusing on God.[46] When the cravings come, people choose to pray in order to grow closer to God and learn self-control.[47]

One of my best friends and his brother participate in a ten day fast every several years. The running joke among the brothers and the rest of us who know them is that one of the brothers uses the time of abstaining from food to pray in order to draw closer to God, whereas the other brother treats the fast as a diet to lose weight. Both benefit from fasting, but for entirely different reasons. One brother gives a report every few days about what God has been teaching him through prayer. The other brother reports about how much weight he has lost.

Though less common than fasting, many Christians over the centuries have used icons to enrich their time of prayer. One of the Ten Commandments forbids worshiping images (Exodus 20). Despite the prohibition, many people have disobeyed this mandate for centuries. Whether we realize it or not, most of our lives are full of images and symbols that point us to things beyond the objects themselves.[48]

My guess is that there are a number of symbols within your daily life (in your room, house, or car, perhaps displayed on your clothing or social media pages). Pause for a moment and look around the space in which you are reading this book. How many images do you notice? What symbols tend to grab your attention? Most people wear clothing containing at least one logo or symbol every day. Along with a growing segment of the population, some of

---

[46] Before considering a fast from food or beverages, everyone should be sure to have a physician or other health care professional provide advice and approval.

[47] See John Piper's *A Hunger for God: Desiring God Through Fasting and Prayer*.

[48] David Morgan. *The Lure of Images: A History of Religion and Visual Media in America*. (New York: Routledge, 2007), 2. Morgan's book does an excellent job explaining the power and significance of images in society.

my closest friends have at least one tattoo. Every car has a symbol representing its brand. All fans like to support their sports teams by wearing apparel with the team logo. Those belonging to a fraternity, sorority, country club, or other social group wear clothing with letters or messaging to display their affiliation on a regular basis. There is nothing wrong with any of this, unless of course we allow an image or anything else to become a type of idol.

A trip to Greece a few years ago caused me to think more deeply about the role that religious symbols can play in our lives. I remember walking into a Greek Orthodox monastery high atop one of the tallest mountains on the Greek island of Patmos and standing near the very spot where the apostle John had received revelation from God nearly two thousand years ago. As I quietly entered the dimly lit monastery, I couldn't help but notice dozens of beautiful icons depicting Jesus, the apostles, and many saints who have gone before us. Prior to that day, the only thoughts I had concerning "icons" were that some Christians worshiped them as idols and that images of that nature were typically utilized by those prone to superstition or idolatry.

However, something happened that particular day that I still have trouble understanding. As I traveled through the chamberlike spaces of the monastery, it seemed as if the saints depicted in the icons were literally watching and encouraging me to pray. The peace that filled my soul brought me first to tears, and then to my knees in prayer. Perhaps this experience is what the author of Hebrews meant by "being surrounded by such a great cloud of witnesses" (Hebrews 12:1). In the days that followed, I read more about how images have enriched the spiritual lives of many Christians over the centuries.

Certainly, symbols and objects can become idols. History provides many examples when indulgences, relics, and other icons were used out of ignorance or in deceptive ways. However, some of these objects can serve as aids to spiritual growth. Some icons can serve as reminders to pray, and also convey the gospel and other biblical stories to those who don't read or have trouble understanding parts of the Bible.

Because the majority of people were illiterate during the earliest centuries following Christ's resurrection, icons became commonplace in many Christian communities. The ichthus (fish symbol) was often used by followers of Christ as a symbol of identification amid a culture suspicious of their beliefs. Occasionally, I have noticed the ichthus symbol affixed to the back of cars, as well as other religious symbols placed in prominent places for all to see.

Our lives are full of symbols. Just as a traffic sign, billboard, or mannequin can point to something beyond itself, certain religious images can serve a similar purpose. Most churches have a cross, stained glass windows, and various other images on display. I have numerous friends who wear cross necklaces and other jewelry containing Christian symbols. Regardless of whether or not a person believes the objects themselves have special power or authority, they can point people to Christ, spark conversations about faith, and serve as reminders of God's promises and the importance of worship.

It is hard not to appreciate the beauty displayed within the art and architecture of many churches throughout the world. I am convinced from experience that the presence of certain religious objects within these sacred spaces can serve as spiritual conversation-starters, point us to scripture, depict biblical events, inspire prayer, and remind us of the Lord's promises and constant presence. Some of my best friends have scripture passages on the walls of each room in their home to serve as a reminder of their identity in Christ and reason for living. Icons continue to be utilized by millions of Christians, especially Catholics, Anglicans, Episcopalians, and members of the Greek Orthodox traditions. Perhaps they may serve as aids to your faith journey as well.

A third helpful aid to prayer is the ACTS acronym. Perhaps you have heard of it. The first letter of each word listed below forms the acronym ACTS. Below are brief instructions about how the ACTS acronym can help guide your time of prayer.

*A*doration - Realizing that you are in the presence of Almighty God, you can love, praise, sing to, worship, revere, and simply enjoy being in communion with your Creator.

*C*onfession - Confess your sins to God and ask him to bring to mind any sins that you cannot remember.

*T*hanksgiving - Because everything we have is a gift from God (life, family, friends, health, and possessions), take a moment to voice (perhaps even write down) what you are grateful for.

*S*upplication - This last word means to ask or petition God for the needs of yourself and others. Because God is the giver of all good things, it is appropriate to ask him for what you need. However, always keep in mind that spending time with God is far better than anything you may desire or receive.

Lastly, take a moment to think about how physical posture can affect your prayers. When really tired I choose to pray sitting up, rather than lying down, because it helps me concentrate and stay awake when praying. Most days, I kneel in gratitude while praying for being able to serve the King of Kings. On occasion, I lift up my hands in praise for the great things God has done in my life, giving thanks for my family, friends, health, and freedom. I have also bowed my head with open hands in anticipation of receiving the wisdom and spiritual strength needed to serve. I have known some people who envision Jesus sitting in a chair across from them while praying. Historically, monks and many other saints have laid prostrate on the floor before the Lord. The key is to discover postures that enable you to stay focused on the ongoing conversation with God.

Questions for Reflection

Do you believe icons or other forms of religious art are useful for some people in their faith journeys? Why or why not?

Is there something you might give up during Lent season or another specific time period of days or weeks so that you can grow closer to God?

What are your thoughts about using the ACTS acronym to guide your prayers?

How might your posture affect your time of daily prayer?

CHAPTER 28
Praying for Healing

I believe in faith healing, not faith healers. By faith healers, I mean persons who possess a supernatural power to heal people at will. God has certainly used individuals to bring about healing in people's lives over the centuries. In modern times they're called medical professionals and have the initials Dr. or MD beside their names. Despite some claiming otherwise, no one but Jesus has the power to heal people anytime and anywhere. This has always been the case. Everyone knows that sometimes people are not healed, despite the level of spiritual maturity or commitment of those praying for healing. Even the apostle Paul was denied his request to be healed three times (2 Corinthians 12:8-10).

Because God has the power to do anything, we would be foolish not to pray for the healing of others. However, there are some things to keep in mind when doing so. When people aren't healed despite fervent prayers for healing, is someone to blame? Was God not capable of healing them? Did the ones praying not pray hard or sincerely enough? Were they lacking in faith? Was there unconfessed sin in their lives? Maybe the prayers offered, no matter how consistent and sincere, were not aligned with God's better plan. I have known many people who put their faith in God and experienced radically changed lives as a result of an illness that was never taken away.

Instead of accepting certain health issues as an inevitable part of life, or that God can refuse to bring physical healing for a greater purpose, some well-meaning people take a different approach. I had a friend who would get upset with her aging father every time he complained about an ailment. After barking at him for not having enough faith in God to heal his sore knees, bad back, or whatever else was plaguing him, she would often quote the following Bible passage to her father: "By his (Christ's) wounds we are healed" (Isaiah 53:5). She would go on to say to him, "If you don't believe this, you'll never get better!" Her interpretation of the passage was that the suffering and death of Jesus can provide anyone physical healing anytime they claim that verse and pray with confidence, no matter the circumstances.

This has been referred to as the "Name It, Claim It" approach to praying for healing. It is a prevalent theme within a movement known as the "Prosperity Gospel," which has also been called the "Health and Wealth Gospel." Adherents to this theology assert that those living obedient lives will be blessed with great health and riches. For those holding to this mentality, what happens when a person dies of old age, like in the case of my friend's father who was 95? At some point physical healing is not possible, and the person dies. The argument cannot shift to "God did heal them, because now they are free of all physical ailments in heaven." This is not what was meant when they were praying for healing. They were praying for God to heal the person here and now, on this earth. While it is in a sense the more complete answer to prayer when God does provide healing at death and in the resurrection, if the "Name It, Claim it" people admit that, they are undoing their whole theology that claims we can and should be healed here, always, because every person does not end up in heaven.

Reading the Bible and studying history prove that the "Name It, Claim It" approach to prayer leaves either God or the people praying to blame when prayers for healing are not answered. This isn't healthy for anyone. Reflecting on the thousands of obedient Christian martyrs over the centuries, as well as the financial and physical hardship faced by countless devout believers along the way, the Health-Wealth Gospel is simply not supported by the scriptures or history. In fact, the Bible states, "Everyone who wants to live a godly life in Christ Jesus will be persecuted" (2 Timothy 3:12). Jesus and the vast majority of his earliest followers suffered greatly, which included both financial hardship and physical pain. Ten of the twelve original disciples died as martyrs. Most of the Church Fathers suffered as well. Even a cursory look at history proves that many of the most influential Christians over the centuries suffered despite their faithful prayers and holy living.

Even though challenges are inevitable, there is always hope because God still conducts the business of miraculous healing. Spiritual healing happens every time a sinner turns to Christ for forgiveness. Physical healings also happen on occasion. What I can't emphasize enough is that sometimes, no matter how many people pray, or how fervently they are praying, physical healing may not happen simply because we are living in a fallen, broken world. God can be glorified whether physical healing takes place or not. I've seen my wife and others healed from cancer, while family and friends, including children, died from it. I've witnessed people being miraculously healed despite doctors and science giving them just days or weeks to live. I've also seen friends and family members die despite doctors claiming that they would live much longer. In each case, we prayed for healing, for God to be glorified through the situation, and for God's will to be done.

When Jesus and the earliest disciples and other believers healed people, it was God who empowered them to do so. Since the time when Jesus walked the earth, God has continued to use faith and prayer as part of his sovereign plan to bring about healing, both physically and spiritually. I have no doubt that God wants us to pray for physical healing. We are also to pray for God's glory and will to be done (Matthew 6:10; 1 Corinthians 10:31). Praying for healing based on scripture assures us that neither God nor the one praying can be blamed when the prayers are not answered as we expect or want them to be answered.

This should in no way impede believers from asking God to heal people from whatever ailments may be plaguing them; after all, God is the great Physician who can do what doctors and medicine cannot. Like a doctor prescribing medicine, the great Physician commands us to pray for whatever we need. Remember God's response to the apostle Paul's request for healing? Three times Paul asked God to take away the "thorn" that was plaguing him, and all three times God said no. We must also learn to embrace God's final response to Paul: "My grace is sufficient for you" (2 Corinthians 12:8-9). God's grace is sufficient for us too!

Though physical healing may not result from our prayers, spiritual encouragement comes from spending time with God, and that is more important than anything else. One can be physically healed time and time again, but never receive the healing necessary to be forgiven for sins and made spiritually whole by God. The Bible mentions that a person may obtain or accomplish all this world has to offer but forfeit their soul (Matthew 26:16).

When it comes to the Church and praying for healing, the Bible has something to say about this topic as well. The Lord's brother, James, wrote, "Is any one of you sick? He should call on the elders of the church to pray over him and anoint him with oil in the name of the Lord. And the prayer offered in faith will make the sick person well" (James 5:13-15). My friend Bob was scheduled for major back surgery after months of physical therapy and endless pain. A healing prayer service was offered at his church twice per month. Bob was a little reluctant to go but decided to join his wife anyway. As his wife and others were fervently praying for healing, Bob looked around the room and wondered if those going forward could somehow be healed? Thoughts of fake healings and charlatans taking advantage of desperate people crossed his mind. Suddenly, Bob felt the Holy Spirit leading him to go forward so the leaders could pray over him. As they were praying, Bob recalls feeling a warm sensation running through his body and peace filling his mind. Bob's pain was gone. A week later he visited his back surgeon to explain what happened. Following X-rays and a thorough examination, the doctor said, "I can't explain it, Bob, but you are healed." Though physical healing is never guaranteed, churches offering services for healing prayer are more likely to experience stories similar to what was just described. Petitioning God for healing is biblical, and God can be trusted to do what is best for his glory as we pray for healing.

At a time when many leaders get distracted by increasing the size of their respective congregations, it is important to remember that a church can be numerically strong but spiritually weak. In the end, praying for spiritual healing matters more than increasing the size of a congregation. As individual members grow spiritually, the spiritual health of the congregation will improve, and the church will likely grow numerically as well.

Questions for Reflection

What are your thoughts about the examples in the Bible about Jesus and others healing people?

Has there been a time when you or someone you know experienced healing?

What are your thoughts about praying for healing?

CHAPTER 29
Praying for Revival

Eighteenth century evangelist George Whitefield once wrote in his journal, "Lord, give me souls to save, or take mine."[49] If we really believe that each person is made to live forever, and that having a personal relationship with God determines one's eternal destination, praying for opportunities to share the love and grace of God with others should be at the top of our daily list of prayers. Every generation has needed revival because every person needs God's forgiveness. As a person hears and responds to the gospel, a revival takes place. The Bible states, "There is rejoicing in the presence of the angels of God over one sinner who repents" (Luke 15:10). Historically, the term "revival" has been used when a group of people turned to Christ for salvation and renewal, which subsequently led to changed behavior, an increase in morality, and greater love for God and others. True revival is always marked by the presence of God. Prayer and repentance prepare the way.

Unfortunately, there can be a negative side to "revivals." Spiritual opposition, charlatans, and various other forms of distraction often attempt to thwart God's work and steal the joy from those who have experienced revival. Even some who initially had pure intentions can

---

[49] *George Whitefield's Journals*. 7th ed. (Carlisle, PN: Banner of Truth Trust, 1998).

succumb to the temptation to manipulate or exaggerate situations in order to receive recognition, monetary gain, or the applause of others. Despite human desires and efforts, true revival begins and ends with God.

Given the times in which we are living, revival is needed today more than ever. The words spoken by legendary singer Bob Dylan decades ago have never rang louder or more true: "Times they are a changin." They are changing indeed, and more rapidly than anyone could have imagined. Increasing numbers are choosing to follow the secular religion of the world. God's name and words are being defamed and undermined, even in some places that used to cherish the Judeo-Christian foundation upon which they were built. Liberties are being taken for granted, and many people think they're being virtuous in their abandonment of biblical values. Sadly, in some Christian contexts it has become increasingly harder to differentiate the Church from the world.

Though the outlook of the world may seem bleak, there is reason for great hope. When I read the scriptures and study the history of Christianity, I am reminded of how far we've drifted, but also how we can return to loving God supremely so that a confused and distracted world might see and embrace God's love and grace. We read in Psalm 85:6 a question asked of God by the psalmist: "Will you not revive us again so that your people may rejoice in you?" Our despair can turn to rejoicing when we turn to God in prayer. Centuries ago, God reminded his people of this truth:

> If my people, who are called by my name, will humble themselves and pray and seek my face and turn from their wicked ways, then will I hear from heaven and will forgive their sin and will heal their land (2 Chronicles 7:14).

God has always desired his people to be prayerful, obedient followers who would spread his healing message of salvation to the ends of the earth. Take a moment to reflect on the instructions given by Jesus to his followers:

> You are the light of the world. A city on a hill cannot be hidden. Neither do people light a lamp and put it under a bowl. Instead, they put it on its stand, and it gives light to everyone in the house. In the same way, let your light shine before men, that they may see your good deeds and praise your Father who is in heaven (Matthew 5:14-16).

Jesus admonishes us to be light. Where is light most evident? That's right! Light is most evident in darkness! As things become spiritually darker, we have a greater opportunity to shine brightly for the Lord! When the early followers of Christ faced challenges, they turned to God in prayer! They cared nothing about programs, surveys, being politically correct, or whom they might offend by proclaiming God's truth and love. The threat of imprisonment or death was very real. Rather than asking for safety, they often prayed for courage to endure. Though frightened, they found unity and peace through prayer. They only wanted people to experience the abundant love, peace, and joy that God had provided them. Despite spiritual and physical opposition, they knew that prayer could unleash God's power and bring true revival.

When Peter, the one chosen by Jesus to lead the early church, was arrested and brought before authorities to explain himself, he said, "We cannot help speaking about what we have seen and heard." Knowing he and the other believers could be killed for their witness, rather than seeking comfort or the approval of others, Peter prayed, "Lord, consider their threats and enable your servants to speak your word with great boldness. Stretch out your hand to heal and perform miraculous signs and wonders through the name of your holy servant Jesus." God empowered them indeed, for the passage goes on to say that, "After they prayed, the place where they were meeting was shaken. And they were all filled with the Holy Spirit and spoke the word of God boldly" (Acts 4:20, 29-31).

Despite the odds, the believers lived, prayed, and died for Christ with great courage. The apostle Peter asked to be crucified upside down on a cross because he felt unworthy to die in the same manner as Jesus. The apostle Paul was beheaded in Rome in the same time period. Every disciple except two were martyred for their faith as well. Countless others died as martyrs in the centuries to follow, for they too could not help but to pray and faithfully proclaim the truth about what they had seen and heard.

Prayer reveals priorities and intentions. The scriptures show us over and over again how God used the prayers of his followers to carry out his purposes and change them in the process (Acts 1:14; 4:31). If believers today plan to live boldly and courageously amid a culture that is becoming increasingly hostile to the name of Jesus being proclaimed, prayerlessness is not an option. You and I simply cannot be the people God intends us to be unless we become prayerful people. Families, communities, and congregations will not be what God intends them to be without prayer. True revival becomes possible when God's people commit themselves to fervent prayer. Lord, please help us to be prayerful.

Questions for Reflection

How did the earliest followers of Christ respond to the challenges of persecution and living in a culture that appeared to care less about God?

Jesus calls his followers to be light. What might this look like in your life and the community in which you live?

CHAPTER 30
Praying with Eternity in Mind

A few years ago, one of my best friends was diagnosed with cancer. James was married with three children between the ages of ten and sixteen. He loved God and his family and was never down about anything. James would often text me passages of scripture and let me know he was praying for me. When I'd visit him in the hospital during chemo treatments he'd laugh, pray, and praise the Lord despite the hell he was enduring. When I asked him one day about how he could have such a great attitude despite the cancer battle, James responded with a quote from C.S. Lewis. In his classic work, *Mere Christianity*, Lewis wrote, "If you read history you will find that the Christians who did the most for the present world were precisely those who thought most of the next." James then said, "Praying helps me to focus on God and eternal things."

I was always encouraged by our visits, so it was a bummer not to be able to visit him during the pandemic. We continued to text and chat on the phone, and then one day I received an unexpected invitation. James called and asked if I could come pick him up so we could eat at our favorite Tex-Mex restaurant. I thought he wasn't able to be around people because of his compromised immune system. When I asked him if he was feeling better, he said, "I'm not worried about getting worse, for they've called in hospice. I want to see you before I die."

Prayerful

I prayed all the way to his house. When I pulled into the driveway and walked past his three kids who were standing outside, I wondered if they knew their dad wouldn't be around much longer. It was a quiet drive to the restaurant as I struggled with what to say. After sitting down and ordering our lunch, James said, "I want to talk about college sports and all the things we love, but first I must share something really important with you. I'm standing on the edge of eternity, and this is the last time you will see me on this side of it. You are standing on the edge of eternity too. It took cancer for me to put things into perspective and understand the value of time. Every day is a gift and opportunity to glorify God. I'm ready for eternity, but many people we know may not be. Promise me that you'll live the rest of your days knowing you are standing on the edge of eternity. Make each day count for the Lord!" James passed away a few weeks later and I had the privilege of praying at his funeral. I am looking forward to seeing him again.

My guess is that you have lost a family member or friend to death. If not, it is only a matter of time. It is a difficult topic that most people don't like to think or talk about, yet everyone will experience it. One day, you and I will stop breathing and die. It is a humbling, sobering thought. What will matter then? What will the people who hear the news of your passing remember about you? How can we have peace about something so inevitable and seemingly grim?

The Bible and history teach us how we can pray through the challenges that come with death. There is no better example than Jesus praying on the evening before his execution. Because his death was fast approaching, Jesus became greatly distressed while praying in the Garden of Gethsemane. Knowing he would be nailed to a cross the following day, Jesus said, "My soul is overwhelmed with sorrow to the point of death." As the burden became too great to bear, Jesus "fell to the ground and prayed" (Mark 14:33-35). This action of falling prostrate on the ground demonstrated complete dependence on and trust in the heavenly Father. For centuries,

Praying with Eternity in Mind

this gesture has been repeated on Good Friday by monks, and also during ordination ceremonies of deacons, priests, and bishops as an expression of complete trust in God while praying.[50]

Given the enormous weight and responsibility of dying as an innocent man in order to take away the sins of humanity, Jesus asked God to remove the burden. It was a natural response given the gravity of the situation, and though Jesus initially wanted to avoid it, he ended up submitting to God's necessary plan. In anguish, Jesus said, "Abba, Father, everything is possible for you. Take this cup from me. Yet not what I will, but what you will" (Mark 14:36). The struggle was real, and Jesus provided us the perfect example of how we should respond to the trials of life. The words, "Not my will, but your will be done, Lord," should be part of our daily prayers as well.

God knows exactly what we are going through at every moment. In our own strength, life can be overwhelming, but with God's help, we can accomplish what God leads us to do. After having been beaten, shipwrecked, and imprisoned on several occasions, the apostle Paul wrote, "I have learned in whatever situation I am to be content. I know how to be brought low, and I know how to abound. In any and every circumstance, I have learned the secret of facing plenty and hunger, abundance and need. I can do all things through Christ who gives me strength" (Philippians 4:11-13). Paul knew that Christ's victory guarantees an eternal crown for everyone who believes. Despite his many hardships, notice how Paul embraced this reality and longed for his eternal reward:

> I will continue to rejoice, for I know that through your prayers and the help given by the Spirit of Jesus Christ, what has happened to me will turn out for my deliverance. I eagerly expect and hope that I will in no way be ashamed, but will

---

[50] Pope Benedict XVI. *A School of Prayer: The Saints Show Us How to Pray*. (San Francisco: Ignatius Press, 2012), 156.

have sufficient courage so that now as always Christ will be exalted in my body, whether by life or by death. For to me, to live is Christ and to die is gain (Philippians 1:18-21).

Trouble is an inevitable part of life, and death will find each of us at some point down the road. God will be with us then, just as he is at every moment of our lives. The difficult times remind us that everything is not as it should be. Unfortunately, for some people, the experiences of this world may be the best they will ever know.

Everyone dies, but not every person will live in the presence of God forever. Sin separates us from God, and if one chooses to reject God's grace the separation will eventually become permanent. This main tenant of Christianity has been upheld for two thousand years. The Bible teaches that people are created in the image of God, and that God has put eternity in the heart of every person (Genesis 3:26, Ecclesiastes 3:11). It is the reason why we long for something beyond what this world can provide. The insatiable desire for something more can only be satisfied by knowing God personally. One can hear the Good News of Jesus dying on a cross and rising from the dead to conquer sin and death so that we can be forgiven, but still choose not to believe it. Because death is inevitable, reaching a peaceful conclusion about what happens at the end of life should be a top priority for everyone.

When we experience the passing of a loved one, the concept of our own mortality becomes much more of a reality. After a lengthy battle with cancer, my grandfather had only a few hours left to live. When I entered the room and stood by his bed, he motioned for me to lean in close so I could hear what he had to say. His voice was weak, and he hadn't said much during the past two days of being in and out of consciousness. As I listened carefully, he pointed to a table across the room and whispered just one word: "Bible." I grabbed his Bible and asked if he wanted me to read something to him. I remember how he had been trying to read it straight through for the first time before he died. The bookmarker was placed near the very end of the Bible, signifying the place where he had stopped reading.

When I asked if he'd like for me to read from the place where he had stopped, he nodded "yes." Surprisingly, but certainly not coincidentally, all that was left to read were the final two chapters of the Book of Revelation. As I read the apostle John's vision of the new heaven and new earth, a big, peaceful smile came across my grandfather's face. I had to pause several times to wipe tears from my eyes as I read John's account that describes what heaven will be like:

> And I heard a loud voice from the throne saying, "Now the dwelling of God is with men, and he will live with them. They will be his people, and God himself will be with them and be their God. He will wipe away every tear from their eyes. There will be no more death or mourning or crying or pain, for the old order of things has passed away" (Rev. 21:3-4).

It was a powerful reminder of God's promise to make everything right. Not just right, but perfect. Those last days of my grandfather's life taught me that we don't have to fear death when we know that Jesus is alive. My grandfather could die in peace because he knew to whom he belonged and where he was going. When death is near, we tend to contemplate what matters most and push aside everything else. We all know at some point life here will not get better. At the same time, we are comforted by the promise that the best is yet to come.

As I stood by his side and prayed for a while, life's three most important questions crossed my mind: Do you know that God loves and cherishes you? Do you understand that Christ's victory over death has pardoned your sins and guaranteed eternal life if you will embrace it? Where do you think you'll go when you die? I had peace about the answers to those questions but realized some people in my life might not.

Prayerful

The value of time is put into perspective when there's not much left. The clock is ticking and somehow seems to go faster as we get older. We are closer to eternity today than we were yesterday. Each day brings us closer. The most comforting truth to embrace when thinking about the end is that at the heart of Christianity is, in fact, the death of someone who has loved us more than we will ever love ourselves. Because Christ died for our sins and was resurrected from the dead, we can live the rest of our lives, and eternity, in the presence of the One who has been through everything we will ever encounter. My grandfather passed away later that day. In the grand scheme of things, you and I are not that far behind.

Made in the USA
Coppell, TX
27 March 2024

30579940R00089